A Great Cloud of Witnesses

16 Saints and Christian Heroes

by

Leo Zanchettin

and

Patricia Mitchell

The Word Among Us
9639 Doctor Perry Road
Ijamsville, Maryland 21754
ISBN: 0-932085-14-8

Second Printing

Cover design by David Crosson
Copy Editor: Laura Worsham

Made and printed in the United States of America.

Table of Contents

Dear Brothers and Sisters in Christ:

Wanting to encourage the people in his church, the author of the letter to the Hebrews reminded them that they were not alone in their desire to give their hearts to Jesus. He told them that they were surrounded by a "so great a cloud of witnesses" and that, therefore, they could continue to "run with perseverance the race" that God had set before them (Hebrews 12:1). These words of encouragement are just as appropriate for us today as they were for the first-century church. In fact, we could probably say that they are *more* true today because we are surrounded by an even greater cloud of witnesses. All of the saints and heroes of Christian history who have gone before us have joined that cloud and forever witness to us of the promise of life in Christ.

What would the people in this "great cloud of witnesses" want to say to us? What words of encouragement would they have for you and me in our everyday lives? We can imagine them crying out with the writer of Hebrews: "Run the race! Stay close to Jesus! Fix your eyes on him! It is possible for you to know the same joy and hope that we know!" They would not testify to something unattainable, something reserved only for a select few. They stand as constant reminders that all things are possible in Jesus. Each in his or her own way shows us what can happen when everyday people take God at his word and allow him to work through them.

Each one of us has been created by God for a specific purpose. He has given us a unique place in his kingdom—a role that no one else can fill—and he delights in empowering us to fulfill this role. The stories of the men and women in this book are wonderful examples of this truth. Their roles were tailor-made for each of them, and God provided them with all the grace and power they needed to fulfill their missions. Though they came from different countries, lived in different eras of history, and had different strengths and weaknesses, they all demonstrated God's faithfulness in pouring out abundant grace on anyone who seeks him.

It is our prayer that the stories in this book—stories of regular people who opened their hearts to Jesus—will move you to embrace with great confidence the life to which God has called you. In Jesus, he has created each of us for something special. Surrounded by this "great cloud of witnesses," may we all come to discover our callings and eagerly run the race that Jesus sets before us. May we all one day join this cloud of witnesses and glorify the God who has loved us from all eternity.

Leo Zanchettin
The Word Among Us

Photo courtesy of the Marians of the Immaculate Conception

Apostle of Mercy

Blessed Sister Faustina

1905 - 1938

Imagine a world where everyone knew God as a loving Father, where no one was bound by guilt or isolation. Imagine a world where all people willingly shared their lives with one another. Imagine a world where everyone had a personal relationship with Christ and where his life radiated from every man and woman. This was the vision that God—early in this century—gave to Sr. Faustina of the Blessed Sacrament, born Helena Kowalska.

Sr. Faustina's vision is especially striking because of the state of the church in her day. Very few people believed that they could experience God and be transformed by him. For many, faith had been reduced to the performance of acts of piety. Many hardened their hearts against a seemingly indifferent God and what looked like a formalized, sterile church. And yet, it was precisely to this church that God sent Sr. Faustina.

Humble Beginnings

Helena Kowalska was born on August 25, 1905, to a poor but pious couple in Lodz, in central Poland. Her father was a carpenter and farmed twelve acres to support his family. Her mother helped on the farm whenever she could, but was mostly busy raising their eight children.

From her youth, Helena was a prayerful child, known for her deep devotion and long nights of prayer. Often, during her night vigils, she would see bright lights that filled her with joy. When at the age of eighteen Helena told her parents that she wanted to enter the convent, they flatly refused. Her housekeeping job helped support the family, and they could not afford the dowry that novices were expected to pay for their wardrobe. Discouraged, she sought comfort in worldly pursuits—more fashionable clothing, an active social life, and other similar distractions. But instead of peace, Sr. Faustina would later write, "The incessant call of grace caused me much anguish."

Helena's impasse finally ended two years later. Her diary records the following:

> I was at a dance with one of my sisters. While everybody was having a good time, my soul was experiencing deep torments. As I began to dance, I suddenly saw Jesus at my side, Jesus racked with pain, stripped of his clothing, all covered with wounds, who spoke these words to me: "How long shall I put up with you and how long will you keep putting me off?" . . . I took a seat by my dear sister, pretending to have a headache. . . . After a while I slipped out unnoticed, leaving my

> sister and all my companions behind and made my way to the Cathedral of Saint Stanislaus Kostka.

At the cathedral, she heard God say, “Go at once to Warsaw; you will enter a convent there.” Helena returned to her uncle’s house, where she was staying, packed a few belongings, and asked her sister to say goodbye to her parents for her. She left most of her clothes behind: “What I am wearing is enough. Jesus will take care of all my needs.”

In Warsaw, she found a job and began her search. But nearly every convent turned her down. Only the Sisters of Our Lady of Mercy would accept her—and then, only after a year’s wait.

Formation and Preparation

Helena entered the convent in August 1925 and took the name Sister Faustina. Faustina means fortunate, or blessed one—and this was how she finally felt. After a peaceful first year, however, she became afflicted with inner turmoil and confusion:

> Darkness began to cast its shadow over my soul. I felt no consolation in prayer; I had to make a great effort to meditate; fear began to sweep over me. Going deeper into myself, I could find nothing but great misery.

For a full eighteen months, she endured such frustrations and temptations, striving all the while to remain faithful to God. In addition to her interior struggles, Sr. Faustina grew physically weaker. This was due, in part, to her inner trials, which sapped her energy. But it was also due to the undetected onset of tuberculosis, the disease that took her life at age thirty-three. She tried with all her will to hide her sufferings, but each time, she would ultimately collapse and need days, even weeks, to regain her strength. Within the convent, Sr. Faustina was the subject of suspicion and mockery. Some accused her of laziness, others of hysteria and delusions.

These trials were not without their purpose, although she could not see it at the time. God was at work purifying her, revealing sin to her so that she would be set free of it and be drawn ever closer to him. Only occasionally did she experience peace or relief from her struggles, but it was always short-lived. God was preparing her for his purposes, forming within her a "broken and contrite heart" (Psalm 51:17), which would be prepared to do his will.

A Mission Revealed

Throughout her life, Sr. Faustina experienced visions of Jesus; her diary often refers to her being "saturated" by God. There was one vision, however, which stood out among all the others, for in this vision, Sr. Faustina's specific calling was made known:

> In the evening [in early 1931] when I was in my cell, I saw the Lord Jesus clothed in a white garment. One hand [was] raised in the gesture of blessing, the other was touching the garment at the breast. From beneath the garment, slightly drawn aside at the breast, there were emanating two large rays, one red, the other pale. In silence I kept my gaze fixed on the Lord; my soul was struck with awe, but also with great joy. After a while,

> Jesus said to me, "Paint an image according to the pattern you see, with the signature: Jesus, I trust in you. I desire that this image be venerated, first in your chapel, and [then] throughout the world. . . . I desire there to be a Feast of Mercy. I want this image . . . to be solemnly blessed on the first Sunday after Easter; that Sunday is to be the Feast of Mercy."

Sr. Faustina did more than produce a painting and ask for a feast of mercy. As time progressed, God invited her to become an "apostle of divine mercy." No one is capable of making reparation to God for sin, but in the history of the church certain people have felt called to share in Jesus' suffering for sin. Such was Sr. Faustina. Christ was calling her to intercede for everyone who had wandered from him or was hardened against him—all those who did not know his love. As she prayed for them, she experienced Jesus' suffering for the ways their sin offended God.

Sr. Faustina's one consolation was that along with her suffering she knew a deep union with Christ, a participation in heaven during her earthly life. Willingly, Sr. Faustina accepted and, from that moment, her mission began:

> My soul became like a stone—dried up, filled with torment and disquiet. All sorts of blasphemies and curses kept pressing upon my ears. Distrust and despair invaded my heart.

At the same time, the love and consolation of Jesus filled her heart. As she contemplated the all-surpassing love of Christ crucified, she grew ever closer to him, eagerly awaiting the day when she would be completely united with him in heaven: "When will you take me to yourself? I've been feeling so ill and I've been waiting for your coming with such longing!"

Promises Fulfilled

Through the help of her confessor, Fr. Sopocko, Sr. Faustina was able to oversee the painting of the image of divine mercy and the celebration of the first Mercy Sunday on April 28, 1935. At the Eastern Gate of Vilnius (now the capital of Lithuania), Fr. Sopocko celebrated a Mass in honor of God's mercy, and the image was displayed before thousands of people. During the Mass, Sr. Faustina had another vision of Christ: The two rays streaming from his heart encompassed the entire world. She was overwhelmed—no one was excluded from mercy. Her only sadness was that the painting did not approach the magnificence of her visions. But Jesus said, "Not in the beauty of the color, nor of the brush lies the greatness of this image, but in my grace."

God so longs to free his people from sin that he sent his Son to redeem us. The rays of light—blood and water flowing from his side—were poured out to pierce the darkness of sin with his forgiveness and new birth. At one point, Jesus told her:

> O, if sinners knew of my mercy, they would not perish in such great numbers. Tell sinful souls not to be afraid to approach me; speak to them of my great mercy. . . . I wait for souls, and they are indifferent toward me. I love them tenderly and sincerely, and they distrust me. I want to lavish my graces on them, and they do not

want to accept them. They treat me as a dead object, whereas my heart is full of love and mercy.

Sr. Faustina lived only three and a half years beyond that first Mercy Sunday, and saw the image of divine mercy receive ever wider recognition. She endured many bouts of inexplicable pain and incapacity as she continued her mission of intercession and her disease slowly overtook her. Finally, after two lengthy hospital stays, Sr. Faustina of the Blessed Sacrament closed her eyes peacefully on October 5, 1938, eagerly awaiting the Lord's embrace.

Apostles of Mercy

Sr. Faustina's experience reveals Jesus as an intimately personal Savior who suffices for every need. Never was she without consolation or direction, difficult though God's will may have seemed. Every moment of doubt faded as she placed her trust in Jesus who had been so merciful to her. Her spirit grew in peace, hope, and confidence, even as her body slowly deteriorated.

Her life was raised up above the darkness and self-centeredness of one bound by the narrow concerns of this world. Through her relationship with Jesus, Sr. Faustina was able to progressively overcome the ways of sin—the selfishness and unbelief that are in all of us—and fix her affections and obedience on Jesus above all else.

All of us are called to know Jesus in a similar way. We can all hear him speak to us as intimately as did Sr. Faustina. We can all know power over sin, progressive victory over behavior patterns that separate us from one another and obscure

God's love in our hearts. We should not consider Jesus and his church as distant, indifferent forces. The word of God can speak to our hearts, his presence can fill our souls, and we can be overcomers in him (Romans 8:37).

God's mercy is immense; no one is excluded from the saving work of the cross. But only those who know they need mercy will reach out for it. Only those who allow the Spirit to show them their sin will realize their need for a Savior. Transformed by his mercy, they will gladly devote their lives to witnessing to the mercy of God. All men and women can become apostles of mercy as they open themselves to the tender mercy and forgiveness of God in Christ Jesus. In this way, the vision God gave to Sr. Faustina can become a living reality for all of us.

On April 18, 1993, Mercy Sunday, Sr. Faustina was beatified by Pope John Paul II in Rome.

Apostle of Mercy

This is a passage from Sister Faustina's diary, written in 1935.

September 29. The Feast of Saint Michael the Archangel. I have become interiorly united with God. His presence penetrates me to my very depths and fills me with peace, joy and amazement. After such moments of prayer, I am filled with strength and an extraordinary courage to suffer and struggle. Nothing terrifies me, even if the whole world should turn against me. All adversities touch only the surface, but they have no entry to the depths, because God, who strengthens me, who fills me, dwells there. All the snares of the enemy are crushed at his footstool. During these moments of union, God sustains me with his might. His might passes on to me and makes me capable of loving him. A soul never reaches this state by its own efforts. At the beginning of this interior grace, I was filled with fright, and I started to give in to it; but very quickly, the Lord let me know how much this displeases him. But it is also he, himself, who sets my fears at rest. (480)

Almost every feast of the Church gives me a deeper knowledge of God and a special grace. That is why I prepare myself for each feast and unite myself closely with the spirit of the Church. What a joy it is to be a faithful child of the Church! Oh, how much I love Holy Church and all those who live in it! I look upon them as living members of Christ, who is their Head. I burn with love for those who love; I suffer with those who suffer. I am consumed with sorrow at the sight of those who are cold and ungrateful; and I then try to have such a love for God that it will make amends for those who do not love him, those who feed their Savior with ingratitude at its worst. (481)

O my God, I am conscious of my mission in the Holy Church. It is my constant endeavor to plead for mercy for the world. I unite myself closely with Jesus and stand before him as an atoning sacrifice on behalf of the world. God will refuse me nothing when I entreat him with the voice of his Son. My sacrifice is nothing in itself, but when I join it to the sacrifice of Jesus Christ, it becomes all-powerful and has the power to appease divine wrath. God loves us in his Son; the painful Passion of the Son of God constantly turns aside the wrath of God. (482)

O God, how I desire that souls come to know you and to see that you have created them because of your unfathomable love. O my Creator and Lord, I feel that I am going to remove the veil of heaven so that earth will not doubt your goodness.

Make of me, Jesus, a pure and agreeable offering before the face of your Father. Jesus, transform me, miserable and sinful as I am, into your own self (for you can do all things), and give me to your eternal Father. I want to become a sacrificial host before you, but an ordinary wafer to people. I want the fragrance of my sacrifice to be known to you alone. O eternal God, an unquenchable fire of supplication for your mercy burns within me. I know and understand that this is my task, here and in eternity. You yourself have told me to speak about this great mercy and about your goodness. (483)

The Life of Sister Faustina

1905 - Born Helena Kowalska on Aug. 25 in the village of Glogowiec, in Lodz County, Poland

1921 - Takes job with another family to help parents

1922 - Parents refuse permission for Helena to enter convent

1924 - Goes to Warsaw with intention to enter religious life

1925 - Accepted into the Congregation of the Sisters of Our Lady of Mercy

1926 - Receives habit and takes the name Sister Mary Faustina

1931 - On Feb. 22, receives a vision of Jesus, who tells her to paint an image of what she sees

1933 - Makes perpetual vows; visions of Jesus continue

1934 - The painting of the image of The Divine Mercy is completed; gravely ill, Sr. Faustina receives the Sacrament of the Anointing of the Sick but recovers

1935 - First Mercy Sunday celebrated on Apr. 28

1936 - Sent to sanatorium for tuberculosis patients in Cracow

1937 - Her health improves, but then deteriorates again

1938 - Dies on Oct. 5

Compelled by Love

Saint Bernard of Clairvaux

1090 - 1153

In the year 1112, a bright young nobleman embarked on an adventure that pioneered new paths—politically, socially, and spiritually—throughout Western Europe. His passion for the gospel and his charismatic personality were so attractive that he drew thirty other men—peers and elders—into the adventure with him. Over the next thirty-five years, hundreds of others would join him on his mission. His advice was sought by kings and popes; he unleashed an international army with the goal of recapturing the Holy Land. He resolved the most complex of disputes between church and state. His sermons and letters on God's love melted the coldest of hearts and endeared him to the most unlikely combination of people—young and old, rich and poor, noble and common. This was the legacy of Bernard of Clairvaux, a Cistercian monk who was both the busiest man of his century and an intensely personal, intimate lover of God.

Bernard was born in 1090 into a noble family in Fontaines, France. His father, Tescelin, was a knight, and all six of his brothers (he had one sister) were expected to follow in their father's footsteps. Bernard, however, showed great intellectual promise, and he was sent to a renowned school at an early age. Both at school and at home, Bernard proved to be an active young man. He read all the literature he could get his hands on, and was always engaging his friends in debates and arguments. Like all the young noblemen of his time, he learned the ways of the court and, while there is no direct testimony, it is likely that he participated in some of the minor wars that were constantly springing up between the different noble families of his region.

A Pioneer

When he was twenty-three years old, Bernard entered the recently founded monastery of Cîteaux, a few miles from his family's castle. So compelling was his anticipation of the new life he was about to embrace that Bernard managed to persuade thirty other noblemen, including his uncle and all of his brothers, to enter as well. Cîteaux was an experimental monastery whose goal was to breathe new life into the venerable Benedictine tradition, and such a prospect must have appealed to these young adventurers. Like the youth of today, the challenge of a new thing, the appeal of pioneering a new way of life, captured their imaginations as they asked how they could best serve God and his church.

Just three years after he entered Cîteaux, Bernard was chosen to lead a group of monks in opening a new monastery in Langres, Champagne. Bernard named the monastery Clairvaux, or "Clear Valley," reversing the tradition of calling the region "The Valley of Bitterness." He was only twenty-five years old, but Bernard's wisdom, his passionate love for God, and his obvious capacity for leadership made him the logical choice.

News of the success at Clairvaux—especially of the young noblemen who joined Bernard—spread, and soon the house was filled to capacity. In 1118, Bernard sent out a band of monks to start a monastery in Châlons. A year later, another group was sent to Dijon, and in 1121, another group went to Soisson. The pace continued throughout his thirty-five year administration, and by the end of his life Bernard was responsible for having founded sixty-eight monasteries, stretching from Scandinavia to Portugal and from England to central Europe.

A Counselor and Diplomat

In every house he founded, Bernard saw to it that the brothers were deeply rooted in Christ through personal prayer, scripture, and the liturgical rhythm of Benedictine life. His primary responsibility was to foster a deep love for Jesus in his brothers so that whatever work they undertook would be marked by humility, wisdom, and gentleness. To this end, he wrote a treatise entitled *On The Steps of Humility and Pride* and *A Letter on Love*, both around the year 1124.

As Bernard's men spread throughout Europe, his influence and reputation grew as well. In 1128, at the request of the

Archbishop of Sens, he wrote another treatise: *On the Conduct and Duties of Bishops*. This was a somewhat risky undertaking, since it had the potential of putting him on the wrong side of the hierarchy. His worst fears went unrealized, however, and Bernard was invited to participate in the Council of Troyes later in that year. From that point, Bernard's place in higher circles of church and state was secured. He alternated his attention between the care of his monasteries and the public arena, all the time preserving and deepening his love for Jesus through his treasured monastic life.

Bernard spent five years trying to resolve a split in the church that had given rise to the election of two rival popes. He crisscrossed Europe preaching the Second Crusade, urging knights and rulers throughout Christendom to fight, not for treasures or land, but out of love for Christ. They were not to give in to the bloodthirstiness that characterized previous wars. Rather, they were to lay down their lives to liberate the Holy Land from the hands of unbelievers. Needless to say, Bernard was deeply saddened by the soldiers' inability to uphold such spiritual aims—the reason, he believed, why the Crusade was a massive failure.

An Active Lover of God

Bernard was an intense man, and he brought this intensity into his relationship with God. Not content simply with reciting prayers and psalms, Bernard wanted to know this God to whom he had dedicated his life. Unless he had experienced God, he felt he could not speak about him. Unless he had experienced God's love, he felt he could not urge others to seek this love.

Bernard's writings testify that his seeking was rewarded far beyond his expectations. Throughout his commentaries and sermons he consistently refers to his own experiences of God, personal and intimate though they were. With as capable and talented a mind as he had, Bernard could easily have focused his attention on the intellectual sphere alone, becoming a noted theologian. But this was never enough. If God is love, then to know God is to know love—living, active, effective. If scripture spoke about Jesus as a bridegroom and a lover seeking his bride, then those who wanted to follow the Lord were invited to experience an embrace of love so intimate that the only human analogy that drew close to it was the union of a husband and wife.

This is the logic behind Bernard's *Sermons on the Song of Songs*, a project he pursued for almost twenty years, even as he kept up with all his other responsibilities. Rather than produce a verse-by-verse commentary, Bernard used this biblical love poem as a pretext for speaking about the way Jesus had won his heart. It is a telling fact that Bernard wrote eighty-six sermons on the Song, yet he only made it up to the first verse of the third chapter!

A Man of Contemplation and Action

For Bernard, it was an ever-deepening encounter with the transforming love of God that gave him the motivation to take up such an active and public life. Even when he threw himself into his roles as diplomat or administrator or arbiter, in his heart was always a desire to return to his home of Clairvaux. More than anything, he treasured his times of intimacy with the Lord, when he could allow the limitless love of his Savior to flood his heart and mind. In one of his sermons on the Song of Songs, Bernard explained this relationship:

> After the Bridegroom has gazed on the soul with kindness and mercy, his voice softly whispers the divine will. His voice is love itself, and love never rests but is continually urging the heart to do God's bidding. The spouse also hears the call to rise up in haste and take up the work of saving souls. The nature of true, pure contemplation is such that, while kindling the heart with divine love, it sometimes fills it with great zeal to win other souls for God. The heart gladly gives up the quiet of contemplation for the work of preaching. Once its desires are fulfilled, the heart quickly returns to contemplation, as to the source of good works. In the same way, once it has tasted anew the delights of contemplation, it joyfully dedicates itself to new works. (57.9)

When he died in 1153, Bernard left behind the witness of a man who was a successful politician, businessman, and diplomat because the man was a successful lover of Christ. As he was filled with God's love, he rightly understood the challenges and demands of his age and responded to them effectively. Increasingly freed from the self-love that is at the root of all sin, Bernard moved beyond his own needs and desires to meet the needs of those around him.

Compelled by Love

The following passage is excerpted from Bernard's *Sermons on the Song of Songs*:

I want to tell you how God has come to me. I have known he was there; I have remembered his presence afterward; sometimes I had an inkling that he was coming. He did not enter by the eyes, for he has no color; nor by the ears, for he made no sound. I could not smell him, for he is not mingled with the air, but the mind. He did not blend into the air; he created it. I could not taste his coming, for he was not eaten or drunk; neither could I touch him for he is impalpable. So how did he come to me?

A curious explorer, I have plumbed my own depths, and he was far deeper than that. If I looked outward, I saw him far beyond. If I looked inward, he was further in still. And I know that what I had read was true, that "in him we live and move and have our being" (Acts 17:28).

How did I know he was present, if his ways cannot be traced? He is life and power, and as soon as he enters in he stirs my sleeping soul. He moves and soothes and pierces my heart, which was as hard as stone and riddled with disease. He begins to root up and destroy, to build and to plant, to water the dry places and light the dark corners, to open what was closed, set what was cold on fire, and to make the crooked straight and the rough places smooth—all so that I can bless the Lord and so that all that is within me might praise his holy name (Psalm 103:1).

When the Bridegroom, Christ the Word, came to me he never made any sign that he was coming; there was no sound of his voice, no glimpse of his face, no footfall. He made no movement by which I could identify his coming; none of my senses showed me that he had flooded the depths of my being. Only by the warmth of my heart did I know that he was there. I knew the power of his might because my guilt and sin were wiped away and my body's yearnings were brought under control.

When God revealed my secret faults, I was amazed at the depth of his wisdom. At the slightest sign of a change of heart, I experienced his goodness and his mercy. As he recreated and renewed the spirit of my mind—the inner man—I perceived the excellence of his glory and his beauty. When I contemplate all these things I am filled with awe at his unending greatness.

To those of you who have experienced this, I say: Enjoy it. To those of you who have not, I say: Burn with desire, that you might come to experience it. We don't perceive his coming in an audible sound, but as the very music of the heart. It is not a sound from the lips, but a stirring of joy. It is not a harmony of voices, but a union of wills. We do not hear it outwardly; it does not sound in public. The only ones who hear him are the one who sings, and the one to whom the song is sung—the Bride and the Bridegroom. It is a wedding song, expressing the embrace of chaste and joyful souls, the harmony of their lives and the mutual exchange of their love.

The Life of Bernard of Clairvaux

1090 - Born at Fontaines

1098 - Monastery at Cîteaux founded

1112 - Accompanied by 30 other noblemen, joins Cîteaux

1115 - Commissioned to found monastery at Clairvaux

1118 - Monastery at Three Fountains founded

1119 - Fontenay founded

1121 - Foigny founded

1124 - Writes *On the Steps of Humility and Pride* and *A Letter on Love*

1128 - Writes *On the Conduct and Duties of Bishops*; attends the Council of Troyes;

1130-1138 - Schism in the Church over rival popes

1135 - Begins writing *Sermons on the Song of Songs*

1139 - Attends Second Lateran Council

1140 - Writes *On the Conversion of Clerics*

1145 - Peter Bernard of Pisa, one of Bernard's monks, elected Pope Eugenius III; Bernard his most trusted advisor

1146-1148 - Helps organize the Second Crusade

1149 - Failure of the Crusade

1153 - Dies on Aug. 20

A Samurai's Noble Death

Saint Paul Miki

1564 - 1597

Paul Miki saw sparkling Nagasaki harbor coming into view. The 600-mile journey from the Japanese capital of Kyoto through the cold and snow was nearly over. It had taken almost one month. Now the crown of martyrdom would soon be his.

Along the road, villagers jeered him and the twenty-three others who had been sentenced to die for their Christian beliefs. "Fools," they shouted, "Renounce your faith." Miki, who loved to preach, urged the people to believe in Jesus, the Savior who died for their sins so that they might live! Not all were insulting the prisoners, however. Fellow believers along the way blessed them, encouraged them, and prayed for them, giving them the strength and courage to continue on their journey.

Miki thought how odd it was that he was to die so soon before his ordination as a priest. Now thirty-three years old, he had been a Jesuit brother for eleven joyful years, studying and internalizing the mysteries of the faith. Recognized as an eloquent speaker, his fervent discourses had led to many conversions. Yet he was never to celebrate Mass, never to raise the consecrated host in his own hands. Perhaps in heaven he would have that privilege.

A Quietly Flourishing Faith

His thoughts on the journey often turned to his family. Miki had been born and raised in the Tsunokuni district near Kyoto in comfortable surroundings, the son of a brave soldier, Miki Handayu. A fellow Jesuit, Francis Xavier, had come to Japan in 1549, and his message of a loving triune God had pierced the souls of many Japanese. In 1568, when Paul was four years old, his parents converted to Christianity. Now there were hundreds of thousands of Christians in Japan, from poor peasants to feudal lords. Miki thought about how lovingly his parents had nurtured his faith. Educated in Jesuit schools, Miki never doubted his vocation.

The seeds planted by Xavier flourished, but only when it suited the reigning Japanese ruler. The military leader Oda Nobunaga allowed the missionaries to preach because he wanted to challenge the power of the Buddhist monks and he was interested in foreign trade. When Nobunaga died in 1582, one of his generals, Toyotomi Hideyoshi, seized power. At first, Hideyoshi tolerated Christianity.

Yet Christianity was a religion of foreigners, very different from Buddhism or the native Shintoism, which enshrined numerous minor gods. Japan feared conquest by the West. What if these foreign missionaries came not to bring their

God but their soldiers? When Christianity began to claim thousands of converts, Hideyoshi became nervous. In 1587, he issued an edict banning all the Jesuit missionaries. The edict was never fully enforced, however, and Miki and his missionary friends continued for a number of years to evangelize unobtrusively.

Blessed Are the Persecuted

Then, in the fall of 1596, a Spanish ship, the *San Felipe*, en route to Mexico from Manila, crashed into the coast of Japan. While Japanese officials confiscated the vessel's cargo, an arrogant remark by the ship's captain was interpreted to mean that missionaries intended to help in the conquest of Japan by Spain. Hideyoshi quickly ordered the arrest of several priests and laymen who had come to Japan from the Spanish Philippines to evangelize. Hideyoshi was firmly convinced that a public, gruesome blood bath would put an end to this religion of the West. Although a native, Miki was among those who would serve as Hideyoshi's warning.

On the day after Christmas in 1596, police came to the Jesuit residence in Osaka. Miki was taken, along with two of his novice brothers, John Soan De Goto and James Kisai. They were brought to a prison in Kyoto, where they were joined by six Franciscans and fifteen members of the Franciscan third order.

A week later, the twenty-four prisoners were led into the public square where the sentence was pronounced: death by crucifixion. Miki's heart soared. What an honor to imitate the Lord on the cross! Each man then stood by the samurai as a portion of his left ear was cut off. It was Miki's turn, and the searing pain shot through his head. The first blood to be spilled for Christ.

The Road to the Cross

As the journey to Nagasaki wore on, Miki became increasingly impatient to be with the Lord. Each day of suffering only increased his longing for God. The words of Psalm 126 echoed in his mind: "He that goes forth weeping, bearing the seed for sowing, will come home with shouts of joy, bringing his sheaves with him." Perhaps his death would sow the seeds of faith in his countrymen. Perhaps his cross would unite with the cross of Christ to bring others to the Father.

At the last stop outside of Nagasaki, two Jesuit priests met the group to hear confessions. Miki poured out his heart. Two more prisoners had joined the group, arrested for trying to comfort the victims. In all, twenty-six would die.

Entering Nagasaki was like coming home to the new Jerusalem. As the caravan entered the city, thousands of faithful Christians lined the streets to encourage the prisoners. Under a feudal lord, Baron Omura, Nagasaki had become a Christian town, with Jesuits running schools, churches, and homes for the poor, even as it flourished in its trade with the Europeans. If Hideyoshi had intended the crucifixions to discourage the Christians here, his plan was already having the opposite effect.

The morning light of February 5—the day of execution—was sharp and unforgivingly bright, like the spears that would soon pierce the prisoners' hearts. Miki and the others were led up Nishizaka Hill, the final mass of land greeting Nagasaki Bay.

The road to Omura divided the hill. One side of the road was scattered with human remains, where common criminals were executed; the other side was covered with new, green wheat. The government official in charge of the executions, Terazawa Hazaburo, had been persuaded by influential Portuguese to give the martyrs a more decent killing field than those of criminals. The wheat would serve as a carpet for their crosses.

A Faithful Samurai

Lying on the ground were the instruments of death—twenty-six crosses, each one tailor-made for the martyrs. When the prisoners saw them, they burst into praise, singing *Te Deum*, the church's traditional hymn of thanksgiving. Three children were among the group of prisoners—thirteen-year-olds Thomas Kozaki and Anthony Deynan, and twelve-year-old Louis Ibaraki—and they raced ahead of the others. The boys, who used to serve the friars at Mass, wanted to find the crosses that fit their small frames. One by one, on their knees, the martyrs embraced their crosses—their way to perfection and to the Father.

The victims were fastened to the crosses with metal bands and ropes. Miki's cross was too big for him, so the guards tied him to the wood with a piece of linen, stepping on his chest in the process. A missionary standing by protested, but Miki assured him: "Let him do his job, Father. It does not really hurt."

The crosses were lifted and slid into holes in the ground, twenty-six stretching in a row from the bay to the road. The martyrs raised their eyes to heaven and sang, "Praise the Lord, ye children of the Lord." The "Sanctus, Sanctus, Sanctus" of the Mass echoed down the hill. Finally, one of the prisoners chanted the litany, "Jesus, Mary. Jesus, Mary." The crowds of Christians joined in. Then, one by one, the men were approached and asked if they wanted to recant their faith in exchange for their lives. Each one loudly answered, "No."

Planted in front of Miki's cross was the death sentence Hideyoshi had declared: "As these men came from the Philippines under the guise of ambassadors, and chose to stay in Kyoto preaching the Christian law which I have severely forbidden all these years, I come to decree that they be put to death, together with the Japanese that have accepted that law." Fastened to his cross, Paul Miki gave his final defense in the form of a samurai farewell song:

> I did not come from the Philippines. I am a Japanese by birth, and a brother of the Society of Jesus. I have committed no crime. The only reason I am condemned to die is that I have taught the gospel of our Lord Jesus Christ. I am happy to die for such a cause and accept death as a great gift from my Lord. At this critical time, when you can rest assured that I will not try to deceive you, I want to stress and make it unmistakably clear that man can find no way to salvation other than the Christian way.
>
> The Christian law commands that we forgive our enemies and those who have wronged us. I must therefore say here that I forgive Hideyoshi and all who took a part in my death. I do not hate Hideyoshi. I would rather have him and all the Japanese become Christians.

The guards listened, spellbound. Miki had shown he could remain a faithful Japanese, adhere to the samurai code of honor, and yet give glory to Christ. Looking to heaven, he said, "Lord, into thy hands I commend my spirit. Come to meet me, ye saints of God."

"Death, Where Is Your Sting?"

The time for execution came. Two samurai guards stood at the foot of each of the crosses at either end of the line of prisoners. In one moment, following the Japanese method of crucifixion, each soldier plunged his steel-tipped bamboo spear into the victim's breast, crossing over each other's spear in the process. First, a guttural yell, then a sudden thrust, then the gush of blood. The heads of the victims sagged. The guards then moved on to the next cross, approaching the center. Miki waited expectantly for the moment when he would meet the Lord.

As the executions continued, an angry roar thundered through the crowd. When the gruesome task was completed, the Christian witnesses broke past the guards, and pressed toward the crosses, soaking pieces of cloth in the martyrs' blood and tearing their clothing for relics. Terazawa finally stopped the onrush, ordering his guards to keep the crowd away.

The bodies remained on the crosses all day, and in the night, a bishop led pilgrims to them, saying a prayer under each body. In death, Miki and his fellow martyrs continued to preach the good news of Christ: "O death, where is your victory? O death, where is your sting?" (1 Corinthians 15:55).

The Legacy of "Resurrection Hill"

In a letter to his superior, Father Francis Calderon, a Jesuit missionary, wrote, "Although thirty-seven days have passed since they were crucified, we still have before our eyes . . . this holy display of the martyrs' bodies, still on their crosses." Father Calderon added:

> I can tell Your Reverence, that these deaths have been a special gift of Divine Providence to this church. Up to now our persecutor had not gone to the extreme of shedding Christian blood. Our teaching therefore had been mostly theoretical, without the corroborating evidence of dying for our Christian faith. But now, seeing by experience these remarkable and most extraordinary deaths, it is beyond belief how much our new Christians have been strengthened, how much encouragement they have received to do the same themselves.

In 1598 an envoy from the Philippines was permitted by Hideyoshi to gather the last remains of the martyrs and their crosses. The Christians planted a tree in each of the holes in the ground left by the crosses, and in the center they built a big cross. Each year, pilgrims made their way to Nishizaka Hill, which they began calling Martyrs' Hill. The plan to exterminate Christianity had backfired. That horrible instrument of execution, the cross, was bringing others closer to the Father.

The story of the courage and faith of the twenty-six martyrs has been faithfully preserved among generations of Christians. In 1862, these martyrs were canonized by Pope

Pius IX. Today, 400 years after their deaths, a church, museum and bronze monument stand atop Nishizaka Hill to commemorate the first twenty-six martyrs and all those faithful Christians who followed them. Pope John Paul II visited the site in 1981 and named it "Resurrection Hill."

On the eve of his execution, thirteen-year-old Thomas Kozaki, who was to die with his father, wrote a farewell letter to his mother. Full of simple yet steadfast faith, the power of this letter, like the power of his cross, has not diminished over the years:

> Dear Mother: Dad and I are going to heaven. There we shall await you. Do not be discouraged even if all the priests are killed. Bear all sorrow for our Lord and do not forget you are now on the true road to heaven. You must not put my smaller brothers in pagan families. Educate them yourself. These are the dying wishes of father and son. Goodbye, Mother dear. Goodbye.

A Samurai's Noble Death

The following is an address given by
Pope John Paul II on February 26, 1981,
on his visit to Nagasaki.

Dear friends:

Today, I want to be one of the many pilgrims who come to the Martyrs' Hill here in Nagasaki, to the place where Christians sealed their fidelity to Christ with the sacrifice of their lives. They triumphed over death in one unsurpassable act of praise to the Lord. In prayerful reflection before the Martyrs' monument, I would like to penetrate the mystery of their lives, to let them speak to me and to the whole Church, and to listen to their message which is still alive after hundreds of years. Like Christ, they were brought close to a place where common criminals were executed. Like Christ, they gave their lives so that we might all believe in the love of the Father, in the saving mission of the Son, in the never-failing guidance of the Holy Spirit. On Nishizaka on February 5, 1597, twenty-six Martyrs testified to the *power of the Cross*; they were the first of a rich harvest of Martyrs, for many more would subsequently hallow this ground with their suffering and death.

"There is no greater love than this: to lay down one's life for one's friends" (John 15:13). "Unless a grain of wheat falls into the earth and dies, it remains alone, but if it dies, it bears much fruit" (John 12:24). Christians died in Nagasaki, but *the Church in Nagasaki did not die*. She had to go underground, and the Christian message was passed from parents to children until the Church came back into the open. Rooted in this Martyrs' Hill, the Church in Nagasaki would grow and bloom, to become an example of faith and fidelity for Christians everywhere, an expression of hope founded in the Risen Christ.

Today, I come to this place as a pilgrim to give thanks to God for the lives and the death of the Martyrs of Nagasaki—for the twenty-six and all the others that followed them—including the newly beatified heroes of Christ's grace. I thank God for the lives of all those, wherever they may be, who suffer for their faith in God, for their allegiance to Christ the Savior, for their fidelity to the Church. Every age—the past, the present and the future—produces, for the edification of all, shining examples of the power that is in Jesus Christ.

Today, I come to the Martyrs' Hill *to bear witness to the primacy of love in the world*. In this holy place, people of all walks of life gave proof that love is stronger than death. They embodied the essence of the Christian message, the spirit of the Beatitudes, so that all who look up to them may be inspired to let their lives be shaped by unselfish love of God and love of neighbor.

Today, I, John Paul II, Bishop of Rome and Successor of Peter, come to Nishizaka to pray that this monument may speak to modern man just as the crosses on this hill spoke to those who were eye-witnesses centuries ago. May this monument speak to the world forever about love, about Christ!

The Life of Paul Miki

1564 - Born in Tokushima near Kyoto

1568 - Parents become Christian

1584 - Enters seminary in Azuchi operated by Jesuits

1586 - Enters Society of Jesus; becomes popular and effective preacher

1587 - Japanese ruler, Hideyoshi, orders all missionaries out of Japan

1596 - Spanish vessel crashes into the coast of Japan in the fall; Miki, who is preparing to enter the priesthood, is arrested on Dec. 26 with two companions at Jesuit residence in Osaka

1597 - Sentenced to death by crucifixion on Jan. 3; begins month-long march to Nagasaki; is executed with twenty-five other Christians on Nishizaka Hill on Feb. 5

Archive Photos

The Innocence of Faith

Saint Bernadette Soubirous

1844 - 1879

The modern tendency to enshrine the human intellect—to the exclusion of the spiritual—was well underway in mid-nineteenth century Europe. Rationalism had become entrenched among the educated elite, many of whom regarded the church and its beliefs as relics of the past. For them, religion was for the poor masses who didn't know better.

Into this secular age, the supernatural burst in a spectacular way. Mary, the mother of Jesus, appeared to a poor, illiterate fourteen-year-old peasant girl in a small French town near the Pyrenees. Even though Bernadette Soubirous was the only one to have seen the Virgin, her visions renewed the faith of the French people and of Catholics all over the world.

The events at Lourdes were a stark rebuttal to the notion that there is no reality beyond the earthly plane. When man had begun to exalt himself and not the Almighty, the Lord worked through a young girl to demonstrate that his mercy is available to all people. He chose an effective witness: Bernadette's humility and utter simplicity disarmed the skeptics. At each turn, the walls of resistance and disbelief that faced the young girl crumbled.

Bernadette was the first child of François and Louise Soubirous, who had operated a mill until they were overcome by financial troubles. By the time Bernadette was fourteen, the family—there were now four children—was living in a single dank room that had once been a jail. The odd jobs her parents found provided barely enough to feed the family. Bernadette went to school irregularly; she didn't even attend enough catechism classes to make her First Communion. Plagued with asthma, Bernadette spent most of her time taking care of her younger siblings. But this was the person the Lord chose to do his work.

The First Vision

On Thursday, February 11, 1858, Bernadette went with her sister and a friend to gather firewood. The two other girls ran ahead of her toward Massabielle, outside Lourdes, and waded through a cold, shallow stream. As Bernadette was sitting down to remove her shoes before crossing the stream, she heard a rustling of trees near a grotto. Glancing over, she saw nothing. Again she heard the noise. This time, she saw a beautiful woman, dressed in a white veil and gown, with a blue sash at her waist. A large rosary was draped over her arm, and on each bare foot was a yellow rose. Bernadette instinctively reached into her pocket for her rosary. As she prayed, the lady moved her own beads through her fingers; then she disappeared.

Bernadette's parents were religious, but they were alarmed at the story of her vision and banned future visits to the grotto. Bernadette, however, was drawn to Massabielle "by an irresistible force," as she later explained. Several days afterward, she returned with some friends and went into ecstasy when she saw the woman again. During a third apparition, Bernadette asked the lady to write down her name. The lady only smiled and asked Bernadette: "Will you do me the favor of coming here for a fortnight?" She then said: "I do not promise to make you happy in this world, but in the next."

For the next two weeks, Bernadette went to the grotto every day; she saw the lady on all but two occasions. Several times, she climbed up toward the grotto on her knees and wept—an act of penance for sinners. During this time, the lady in the vision revealed three secrets to Bernadette and gave her a prayer to say every day. Bernadette never told anyone what these secrets were or what she prayed.

As news of the apparitions spread, crowds began to gather, drawn by a palpable sense of the divine. There was no shortage of skeptics, however, including the civil authorities, who feared public unrest. Bernadette was ordered to see the police superintendent, who grilled her about her visions. She remained undaunted. "You can do what you want, sir," she told him when he threatened her with jail.

Finding the Spring

On Thursday, February 25, many of those watching Bernadette thought she had gone mad. They saw her look for something, first in the grotto and then toward the Gave River. The lady had told her to wash in the spring, but she could find no spring. Bernadette later explained: "She pointed with her finger to [the place of] the spring. I went there. I saw merely a bit of dirty water; I put my hand in it, but I could not get hold of any. I scratched and the water came, but muddy. Three times I threw it away; the fourth time I was able to drink some." The next day, people found, at the spot where Bernadette had muddied her face, a spring flowing with clear water.

The lady in the apparition had a specific mission for Bernadette: She was to ask the priests to build a chapel at Massabielle and to allow the faithful to come to the grotto in procession. Obedient to her instructions, Bernadette approached the parish priest of Lourdes. When she told Abbé Dominique Peyramale of the lady's request, he retorted, "What! A lady who goes and perches on a rock! A lady you do not know! A lady who is perhaps as lunatic as you!" Bernadette would at least have to find out the lady's name, the priest said.

The clergy's "wait and see" attitude, however, did not stem the fervor that was growing over the apparitions. On March 4—the last day of the fortnight—there were 20,000 people present and police were stationed along the way to supervise the crowds.

The Immaculate Conception

For three weeks, Bernadette felt no pull toward the grotto. Then on March 25, the Feast of the Annunciation, she felt called to return. This time, she was determined to find out the lady's name. On the first two attempts, the lady only smiled, but when Bernadette persisted, she said: "I am the Immaculate Conception." All the way back to town, Bernadette repeated these words to herself so she would not forget them. She had no idea what they meant, but three years earlier Pope Pius IX had defined this term as an article of faith: Mary was, from the first instant of her conception, preserved from the stain of original sin.

Determined to put a stop to the whole business, the civil authorities conspired to have Bernadette hospitalized. Three doctors who examined her, however, were unable to diagnose mental instability; they found the young girl to be pleasant and intelligent. Since science precluded a supernatural explanation, they decided that a "brain lesion" must have caused the visions. By now, however, Abbé Peyramale had come to believe in Bernadette's apparitions. The proof was in the faith of the people, who were crowding his church for the sacraments. He warned the mayor not to touch a hair on the child's head.

Two more times, Bernadette saw Mary—the last occasion on July 16. Then the apparitions ceased. Four years later, a bishop's commission declared that the Mother of God had truly appeared to the girl, and work on a chapel was begun. Regular processions were held, and streams of visitors made their way to the miraculous spring for spiritual and physical healing. It seemed that Bernadette had accomplished her mission.

Through it all, Bernadette remained humble and unaffected. The constant parade of visitors must have been exhausting, but Bernadette patiently answered their questions. She and her family refused the many offers of money and gifts. When she discovered that photographs of herself were being sold for ten centimes, she observed: "That's more than I'm worth."

Bernadette was now faced with the decision about how to live the rest of her life. Abbé Peyramale had arranged for her to become a boarder at a school in Lourdes run by the Sisters of Nevers, a diocesan community which—despite her poor health—the local bishop eventually invited her to join. At twenty-two years of age, she traveled to the motherhouse in Nevers to begin her novitiate. Even though she found it difficult to say goodbye to family and friends, Bernadette was overjoyed at the prospect of living a quiet, prayerful life.

The Religious Life

The Virgin's prophecy must have echoed in her mind many times as continual bouts of painful illnesses clouded her joy. What Bernadette did not expect was the harsh treatment she would receive from her religious superiors. They had decided in advance that she needed stinging rebukes and a cold shoulder to prevent her from becoming spiritually prideful.

Bernadette's novice-mistress, Mother Marie-Therese Vauzou, seemed to be bothered by the fact that the Lord had chosen a country girl from the lower classes to be his instrument. Perhaps she had expected Bernadette to divulge the secrets she had received from Mary. Bernadette, however, continued to withhold this information, which probably irked the novice-mistress even more. Bernadette was continually told that she was "good for nothing."

After her profession, Bernadette was assigned to the infirmary, where for five years she nursed her sick sisters until her own failing health forced her to become a patient. Another burden was the stream of visitors: Even though the bishop had promised to allow only a few, there were more than enough to try Bernadette's patience.

As her bodily suffering increased—a painful tumor on her knee eventually kept her bedridden—Bernadette worried that she had not profited enough from the graces she had received in her lifetime. She seemed to be experiencing a spiritual darkness. In one letter to her cousin in 1875, she wrote, "Ask our Lord to be so kind as to give me a tiny spark of his love. If only you knew how much I need it!"

Her pain was excruciating in the months before she died, and sleepless nights left her exhausted. Finally, on April 16, 1879, at the age of thirty-five, Bernadette died. Years later, during the canonization process, Bernadette's remains were exhumed and were found to be perfectly preserved. Even in death, the Lord used Bernadette to show his power and glory.

The little town of Lourdes has become synonymous with God's gift of healing; a wall covered with crutches and wheelchairs attests to this. Nearly 150 years later, millions of pilgrims still come to this small corner of the earth to bathe in the "living waters" discovered by Bernadette.

The Innocence of Faith

The following is an eyewitness testimony of Bernadette in the presence of Mary by Jean-Baptiste Estrade, a resident of Lourdes who initially was skeptical of her story.

Bernadette knelt down, pulled out her rosary from her pocket, and made a profound reverence. . . .While slipping the first few beads through her fingers, she raised her eyes to the rock in a searching gaze that betrayed her impatient longings.

Suddenly, as though a flash of lightning had struck her, she gave a start of amazement, and seemed to be born into another life. Her eyes lighted up and sparkled; seraphic smiles played on her lips; an indefinable grace spread over her whole being. From within the narrow prison of the flesh, the visionary's soul seemed to be striving to show itself outwardly and proclaim its jubilation. Bernadette was no longer Bernadette! . . .

Spontaneously we men who were present uncovered our heads and bent our knees like the humblest woman. The time for argument was past, and we, like all those present at this heavenly scene, were gazing from the ecstatic girl to the rock, and from the rock to the ecstatic. We saw nothing, we heard nothing, needless to say; but what we could see and comprehend was that a conversation had begun between the mysterious Lady and the child whom we had before our eyes.

After the first transports caused by the Lady's arrival, the visionary took up the attitude of a listener. Her face and her gestures reproduced all the phases of a conversation. By turns laughing or serious, Bernadette showed approval with a nod of the head, or seemed herself to be asking questions. When the

Lady was speaking, she thrilled with happiness; on the other hand when she herself was speaking and making her petitions, she would bow down to the ground and be moved to tears . . . .

Usually the ecstatic ended her prayers with a profound reverence to the hidden Lady. I have moved much in society, perhaps too much, and I have encountered models of elegance and distinction; but never have I seen anyone make a bow with such grace and refinement as did Bernadette.

During the ecstasy the child also made the sign of the cross from time to time, and, as I said myself on the way back from the grotto, if the sign of the cross is made in heaven, it can only be made in that manner.

The ecstasy lasted for about an hour. Towards the end the visionary moved, still on her knees, from the spot where she was praying to right underneath the eglantine which was hanging down low from the rock. There she recollected herself as if for an act of homage, kissed the ground and returned still on her knees to the spot which she had just left. Her face lit up with a last splendor; then gradually, without any sudden jerk, but almost imperceptibly, the rapture faded and finally disappeared.

The visionary continued praying for a few moments longer, but now all we could see was the pleasant but rustic face of the Soubirous girl. . . .

The Lady of the rock had veiled herself in vain; I had felt her presence and I was convinced that her motherly gaze had hovered over my head. It was a most solemn hour of my life! I was thrown almost into a delirium of madness by the thought that a cynical, sneering, self-satisfied fellow like me had been permitted to come so close to the Queen of Heaven.

The Life of Bernadette Soubirous

1844 - Born in Lourdes on Jan. 7, the eldest child of Louise and Francois Soubirous

1856 - Her family, suffering financial losses, moves to small home that had once been a jail

1858 - *Feb. 11:* Sees first apparition of Mary
Feb. 18: Sees third apparition; Mary asks her to come for a fortnight
Feb. 25: Discovers spring
Mar. 4: 20,000 people come to grotto to see Bernadette; fortnight ends
Mar. 25: Mary identifies herself as the "Immaculate Conception"
Jul. 16: Last apparition

1860 - Moves into Lourdes school and hospice

1866 - Leaves Lourdes and arrives at the Sisters of Nevers Motherhouse. Takes novice's habit and the name Sister Marie-Bernard on Jul. 29

1867 - Makes her religious profession and becomes nurse in infirmary

1873 - Relieved of duties in infirmary due to illness

1875 - Begins life as an invalid

1878 - Takes perpetual vows

1879 - Dies on Apr. 16

Archive Photos

With Christ in the World

Dietrich Bonhoeffer

1906 - 1945

Monday, April 9, 1945: The Allied military forces were continuing to advance deeper into the heartland of Germany. At the same time, in a Nazi concentration camp behind the battle lines, a German doctor was witnessing a martyrdom. Ten years later, the event still vivid in his memory, he wrote:

> I saw Pastor Bonhoeffer . . . kneeling on the floor praying fervently to God. I was most deeply moved by the way this lovable man prayed, so devout and so certain that God heard his prayer. At the place of execution, he again said a short prayer and then climbed the few steps to the gallows, brave and composed. His death ensued after a few seconds. In the almost fifty years that I worked as a doctor, I have hardly ever seen a man die so entirely submissive to the will of God.

The doctor witnessed the death of Dietrich Bonhoeffer, a German Lutheran minister and a great Christian hero of this century. Bonhoeffer, a pastor and theologian, was arrested and tried for smuggling Jews out of Germany and was executed for conspiracy.

First Steps on a Fateful Path

Dietrich Bonhoeffer was born on February 4, 1906, into a wealthy and prestigious family. His father was a leading psychiatrist and university professor in Berlin. His mother came from a family of theologians, preachers, and military and government leaders. He and his seven brothers and sisters were raised in an intellectual environment that encouraged independent thought.

Their career choices were ambitious: Karl-Friedrich, the eldest, for example, studied chemistry and eventually became a university professor; Klaus, another brother, studied international law and held a position in the League of Nations and later in Germany's post-World War I government. Dietrich's brothers were disappointed by his decision to pursue theology and hopefully to serve as a pastor in some quiet village. He was an intelligent young man, with a promising future. Why choose obscurity?

But his mind was made up, and so in 1923, Dietrich began his university studies, eventually studying at Tübingen, Rome, Berlin, and New York. He focused his study on the church and the question: "Who is Jesus Christ for us today?"

As the depth of this question shows, Dietrich Bonhoeffer had inherited his family's ambitious nature. In fact, he approached every task with an aggression that impressed many who knew him. This was true, whether it was rehearsing piano and performing classical music with his family, competing in track-and-field events at school, or engaging in heated discussions with friends. He inherited from his parents the strong build and energetic movements that would characterize his whole life; and with his blond hair, strong brow, and sharp blue eyes, his outward appearance and actions corresponded with the inner intensity with which he worked.

Not surprisingly, Bonhoeffer showed himself suited to rigorous theological work from the start, but was torn between the academic life, which his professors encouraged him to pursue, and the parish life, which so attracted him. Upon ordination as a Lutheran minister in 1931, he chose a demanding combination of both roles, ministering in a church in Berlin's poorer northern district and lecturing at the University of Berlin.

The Gathering Storm

The 1920s and early 1930s were difficult for Germany. The harsh provisions of the Treaty of Versailles—which ended World War I—placed complete responsibility for the war on Germany's shoulders. Coupled with the ravages of a ruined economy and a severe depression, the country had been reduced to political and economic shambles. The people were looking for new leadership that could give them hope. Communists, nationalists, and other political hopefuls were all vying for popular support, especially from the nation's youth.

No movement was more seductive or more ruthless than the National Socialist German Workers' Party (the Nazis), with their cry for a united, strong nation that could shape its own destiny. The Nazis insisted that Germany could achieve this destiny only if she were cleansed of all her internal enemies. This message struck a sympathetic chord in this downtrodden people, and the Nazis grew in popularity and power.

Bonhoeffer saw from the beginning the threat that Nazism posed, and it was not long before he began to see the power of its influence. In 1928, a movement among German Lutherans called the German Christian Church began, seeking to unite all Lutherans together for the renewal of church and country. Aligning itself with the Nazis and calling for a purified Germany, this movement became the official expression of Lutheranism in Germany after Hitler came to power in 1933.

As Bonhoeffer saw the dangers of the German Christian Church, he became involved with an opposing movement among German Lutherans called the Confessing Church. As the name suggests, their primary concern was for a pure confession of faith, free from the dictates and philosophies of current political movements and ideas. With other members of this church, Bonhoeffer drafted such a confession, which revealed his church's clear opposition to the German Christians. Bonhoeffer thus entered the public eye—in a way that was to put him in jeopardy.

The Cost of Discipleship

As the situation in Germany became more grave, the Confessing Church became more active. In 1935, Bonhoeffer established and ran a seminary for the church in the town of Finkenwalde, where he wrote his best-known book, *The Cost of Discipleship*, a series of meditations on the Sermon on the Mount (Matthew 5-7).

In this work, Bonhoeffer distinguished between what he called "cheap grace" and "costly grace":

> Cheap grace is the preaching of forgiveness without requiring repentance, baptism without church discipline, Communion without confession, absolution without personal confession. Cheap grace is grace without discipleship, grace without the cross, grace without Jesus Christ, living and incarnate.

Costly grace, on the other hand, accepts the fullness of the gospel message: love and forgiveness coupled with the knowledge of a sinful human nature which, on its own, cannot stand before God. Costly grace

> . . . is *costly* because it calls us to follow, and it is grace because it calls us to follow *Jesus Christ*. . . . It is costly because it condemns sin, and grace because it justifies the sinner. Above all, it is *costly* because it cost God the life of his Son. . . . Above all, it is *grace* because God did not reckon his Son too dear a price to pay for our life, but delivered him up for us.

Modeling his seminary after the monastic tradition, Bonhoeffer fostered a community of sorts. The men lived a common lifestyle, praying together, confessing their sins to one another, and sharing their insights on the scriptures. Bonhoeffer shared all aspects of their lives, including the games of soccer that followed study and classes. He taught the entire curriculum, and every Saturday he addressed them as their pastor, often speaking from *The Cost of Discipleship*. During this time, Bonhoeffer also wrote *Life Together*, a small book on Christian community, which reflects the seminarians' life at Finkenwalde. The Confessing Church was beginning to grow and to stem the tide of compromised Lutheranism in Germany.

The Doors Are Closed

In 1937, however, the Nazis—having grown more powerful—ordered the seminary closed. During that summer, many of its students were subjected to interrogations, confiscations, and even arrest. The Nazi regime, preparing for war, was silencing all voices of opposition.

Bonhoeffer managed to keep in touch with his students, even illegally establishing some of them in churches as pastoral trainees. In this way, he continued their formation and kept the Confessing Church from being eradicated. Their training, however, came to an end by 1940, when most of them were drafted into the *Wehrmacht*.

As the Nazis moved his country closer to war, Bonhoeffer became increasingly concerned for the nation and especially for the safety of German Jews. The Nazis' official actions against the Jews had begun with the restrictive "Aryan Clauses" of 1933—lowering all Jews to second-class citizenship. The government began its open campaign of terror on November 9, 1938, with the infamous *Kristallnacht* (Crystal Night), a night of beatings and destruction. Shortly afterwards, the Nazis started deporting Jews to concentration camps.

Passive or Active?

Bonhoeffer had to act. Through his family, he met certain men in German intelligence and senior military positions who had formed a resistance group to overthrow the Nazis. Dietrich was repulsed by the thought of deception and violence, but his conscience would not allow him to sit idly by and allow the evil to go on unchecked. But, how far should he go in fighting oppression? Could he actually bring himself to work for his nation's defeat in another war? Dietrich had received invitations to teach theology in New York. Perhaps he should leave Germany altogether to avoid answering such haunting questions.

He decided to go, and on June 2, 1939, left for New York. It proved to be a very short stay. He wrote to his friend Reinhold Niebuhr:

> I have made a mistake coming to America. . . . I will have no right to participate in the reconstruction of Christian life in Germany after the war if I do not share the trials of this time with my people. . . . Christians in Germany will face the terrible alternative of either willing the defeat of their nation in order that Christian civilization may survive, or willing the victory of their nation and thereby destroying our civilization. I know which of these alternatives I must choose; but I cannot make the choice in security!

Abandoning his sanctuary, Bonhoeffer returned to Berlin on July 27. On September 1, 1939, Germany invaded Poland and two days later, Britain declared war.

Conspiracy, Prison, and Sacrifice

As he prayed for divine guidance, Bonhoeffer knew he could not settle for "cheap grace." He committed himself to action. Using his family's influence, he obtained a position in Germany's counter-intelligence agency, the leaders of which were secretly involved in the resistance.

He began by helping to smuggle Jews out of Germany. Over time, he became involved in plans to assassinate Hitler and overthrow the government. His two main roles were to maintain secret lines of communication within the resistance movement and to help plan for a new order in Germany once the current regime was toppled. He spent nearly four years with this work, all the while helping to smuggle Jews out of the country.

In October 1942, the Gestapo uncovered the smuggling operation, and on April 5, 1943, Bonhoeffer was arrested for his part in it. The Gestapo had not yet found anything to connect him to a larger conspiracy. Bonhoeffer was taken to Tegel Prison in Berlin where his trial dragged on for eighteen months. Throughout this time, he maintained correspondence with family and friends. These letters show his intense devotion to Christ, his concern for others, and a lack of self-pity or anger.

Dietrich wrote most frequently to Eberhard Bethge, the husband of his niece Renate and once his student at Finkenwalde. Bethge had joined the military, but was secretly working with the conspirators. It was to him that Bonhoeffer confided his more private thoughts about prison life, as well as the impact his experiences had on his understanding of his relationship to God.

After the July 20, 1944, attempt on Hitler's life, key documents of the conspirators were discovered, and Bonhoeffer's role in the resistance came to light. He was transferred to the Gestapo prison, where he was interrogated more directly. As the Allied forces continued to advance, Dietrich was transferred to three different concentration camps, ending up in Flossenburg in the south. In early 1945, facing imminent defeat, Hitler ordered that no conspirator was to survive. A few days before Allied forces liberated Flossenburg, Dietrich Bonhoeffer was hanged.

A New Theology

Everything that Dietrich Bonhoeffer said and did revolved around the question: "Who is Jesus Christ for us today?" As he asked this question, he began to see how dangerous "religion" could be to Christianity. He saw how religious people tend to restrict God to the outer limits of life, where humanity is confronted by its weaknesses: death, illness, and moral failings. But Bonhoeffer insisted that God is more than just the answer to problems and weaknesses. "The church stands, not at the boundaries where human powers give out, but in the middle of the village."

Rather than exile Christ to the periphery of life, where he becomes man's medicine but not his life's blood, Bonhoeffer saw that Jesus belongs directly in the center, right in the middle of the world:

> The . . . Christian hope of resurrection . . . sends a man back to his own life on earth in a wholly new way which is even more sharply defined than it is in the

> Old Testament. The Christian . . . has no last line of escape available from earthly tasks and difficulties into the eternal, but, like Christ himself, he must drink the earthly cup to the dregs. . . . This world must not be prematurely written off. . . . Christ takes hold of a man at the centre of his life.

A Lived-Out Theology

Faced with glaring manifestations of sin all around him, Dietrich began to understand that salvation in Christ is meant to transform our lives here and now, not only to give us hope for a resurrection to a better life: "It is true that encounter with Jesus meant the reversal of all human values." Jesus belongs at the center of our lives, redefining our concepts of this world and teaching us to live here on earth as he did—as men and women of the world who bring the fullness of the gospel into the world with us.

This belief cost Bonhoeffer his freedom and ultimately his life. He knew he could not accept a "religious" explanation for the Nazi atrocities and serenely await an other-worldly redemption from the evil that was all around him. He had to do everything this faith demanded, taking responsibility for the sins of his people and even sacrificing himself in an effort to right their wrongs.

One month after the failed assassination attempt, Bonhoeffer wrote to Bethge:

> Please don't ever get anxious or worried about me, but don't forget to pray for me—I'm sure you don't! . . . My past life is brim-full of God's goodness, and my sins are covered by the forgiving love of Christ crucified. I'm

most thankful for the people I have met, and I only hope that they never have to grieve about me, but that they, too, will always be certain of, and thankful for, God's mercy and forgiveness.

With Christ in the World 

Dietrich Bonhoeffer wrote this letter to his close friend Eberhard Bethge from Tegel Prison in Berlin on December 22, 1943. (*Maria is Dietrich's fiancée.*)

They seem to have made up their minds that I'm not to be with you for Christmas, though no one ventures to tell me so. I wonder why; do they think I'm so easily upset? Or do they think it kinder to lull me from day to day with empty hopes? . . . The English have a very suitable word for this sort of thing—"tantalizing." Out of pure sympathy they've been "tantalizing" Maria and me for a couple of weeks. . . .

Aren't there things like purification plants in lakes? You know my technical naiveté—but there is something like that, and that's what you are to me. I do want to convey to you somehow tomorrow that my attitude towards my case is unquestionably one of faith, and I feel that it has become too much a matter of calculation and foresight. I'm not so much concerned about the rather artless question whether I shall be home for Christmas or not; I think I could willingly renounce that, if I could do so "in faith," knowing that it was inevitable. I can (I hope) bear all things "in faith," even my condemnation, and even the other consequences that I fear (Psalm 18:29); but to be anxiously looking ahead wears one down. Don't worry about me if something worse happens. Others of the brethren have already been through that. But faithless vacillation, endless deliberation without action, refusal to take any risks—that's a real danger. I must be able to know for certain that I am in God's hands, not in men's. Then everything becomes easy, even the severest privation. Now it's not a matter (I think I can say this truthfully) of my being "understandably impatient," as people are probably saying, but of my facing everything in faith. In this regard, enemies are often much less dangerous than good friends. And I feel that you're the only one who understands that. I think that Maria, too, already feels rather the same thing. If you think of me, in the next days and weeks, please do so in this way (Psalm 60:12). And if you've something to say to me about it, be so good as to write it to me. I don't want to go through this affair without faith. . . .

Now I want to assure you that I haven't for a moment regretted coming back in 1939—nor any of the consequences, either. I knew quite well what I was doing, and I acted with a clear conscience. I've no wish to cross out of my life anything that has happened since. . . . And I regard my being kept here (do you remember that I prophesied to you last March about what the year would bring?) as being involved in Germany's fate, as I was resolved to be. I don't look back on the past and accept the present reproachfully, but I don't want the machinations of men to make me waver. All we can do is to live in assurance and faith—you out there with the soldiers, and I in my cell. — I've just come across this in the *Imitation of Christ: Custodi diligenter cellam taum, et custodiet te.* "Take good care of your cell, and it will take care of you" — May God keep us in faith.

The Life of Dietrich Bonhoeffer

1906 - Born on Feb. 4 in Breslau, Germany

1912 - The family moves to Berlin

1923-1929 - Studies theology at Tübingen, Rome, Berlin, and New York

1931 - Ordained a Lutheran minister; teaches at Berlin University; pastors a church in the city

1933 - Leaves Germany to pastor two churches in London; becomes active in the Christian ecumenical movement

1935 - Returns to Germany and becomes a leader in the Confessing Church while establishing and directing a seminary; writes his best-known book, *The Cost of Discipleship*

1937 - The Nazi regime shuts the seminary down

1939 - Leaves Germany for New York, but returns in three months

1939-1943 - Obtains a position in Germany's counter-intelligence and becomes active in the resistance movement

1943 - Arrested on Apr. 5 and imprisoned in Berlin

1944 - Transferred to a Gestapo prison

1945 - Transferred to three different concentration camps; executed at Flossenburg on Apr. 9

The Heavenly Pilgrim

Saint Francis Xavier

1506 - 1552

The *Santiago* had been stalled for 40 days, blistering under a relentless sun, without so much as a breeze to set it back on its course around the Cape of Good Hope and up to India. The food was rotting, the water was scarce, and many of the passengers were giving up.

Among the hopeless, however, stood a man of great hope: Father Francis de Jassu y Xavier was going to India to reap souls for heaven. In his tattered cassock, the priest labored tirelessly, tending to the sick on board. Francis said later that the trials of the year-long journey were such that "for the whole world, I would not dare face them for a single day." Yet all found comfort—and Christ—in his ready smile, his kindness, his loving acceptance.

As a highly educated Basque nobleman, Francis probably never imagined that one day he would undertake a dangerous sea voyage halfway around the world in a ship full of fortune seekers. Born in 1506 in Navarre, Francis was the youngest of six children. A promising scholar and athlete, he went to study at the University of Paris when he was nineteen years old. War had taken its toll on the family finances, and Francis lived in near poverty in Paris, where he roomed with a former Basque military official, Ignatius of Loyola. A bad leg injury had led Ignatius to a profound conversion.

Francis—tall and athletic, handsome and ambitious—was quite the opposite of his roommate. He looked on Ignatius, who was fifteen years older, with scorn and derision. "He could scarcely set eyes on him without making sport of his plans," a fellow Jesuit, Juan de Polanco, later said of Francis' attitude. Ignatius remained undaunted. He drummed up students for Francis' lectures, lent him money when he was in need, praised and encouraged him.

One day, when Francis was telling him about his plans for a great career in the church—he had been offered a canonry in the Cathedral of Pamplona—Ignatius asked him, "And what shall it profit a man if he gain the whole world and lose his own soul?" It was the question that would transform Francis and the rest of his life. In 1534, on August 15—the Feast of the Assumption—Ignatius, Francis, and five other men went to a chapel in Montmartre, near Paris, where they vowed to go to Jerusalem and to give up their families and all worldly goods. Ignatius' Spiritual Exercises—which would be used by countless others for centuries to come—had led them to make a radical break from the world and to give all their energy, all their gifts, and all their love to Christ. Their work would spark reform in the church at large.

A year later, Ignatius journeyed to Spain, stopping off at the home of Francis' brother carrying a letter of introduction that expressed Francis' great regard and affection for his mentor:

> I give you my word that never in all my life will I be able to repay the debt I owe to him [Ignatius]. Over and over again, both with his purse and through his friends, he has provided for my needs; and thanks to him also I have withdrawn from bad company. . . . I beg you to receive him as you would me. . . . You can learn of my needs and hardships from him better than anyone else, for he knows them better than anyone.

In 1536, Francis left Paris for Italy with eight others who had taken vows at Montmartre. When it proved impossible to get to Jerusalem, they decided to serve at the will of the Pope as the Society of Jesus and were ordained priests in 1537. The men lodged in local hospitals, where they cared for the sick and preached—in bad Italian—on the streets. Ignatius gave his Exercises to others, and the influence of the group began to grow.

Two men from the Society were to be sent to Portugal to prepare for missionary work in the Portuguese territories in India. When one of the men who was to go fell ill, Ignatius asked Francis, his personal secretary at the time, to replace him. "Good!" replied Francis immediately. "I am here and ready." The separation, however, was a sacrifice for both men. Francis wrote later to Ignatius, "I believe that in this life we cannot see each other any more except by letters. To see each other face to face with many embracings—that will be for the other life."

Cape Comorin

Francis arrived in the city of Goa, India, in the spring of 1542. His reputation and popularity grew quickly. Lines formed before his confessional and crowds came to hear his sermons. He befriended those living in obvious sin by inviting himself to dinner, talking easily and knowledgeably about a wide variety of subjects, and then finally calling on them to look at the state of their spiritual lives. Many people in Goa began to refer to him as "the heavenly Pilgrim" or "el Santo."

In September 1542, the colonial governor sent Francis to the bare, windswept lands of Cape Comorin, 600 miles from Goa, where the people made a meager living by pearl fishing. Francis, using a method that he would employ in other lands, found some natives who knew a smattering of Portuguese and, with their help, put together the basic tenets of a catechism in the native language. Twice a day, he gathered the people and taught them. Some days, Francis performed so many baptisms that his hands became numb and his voice faded. In his letters to Ignatius, he begged for more missionaries.

Despite his successes, Francis saw much of his work undone. At one point, nearby tribesmen plundered—and nearly destroyed—the Christian communities he had been building. The people were continually exploited by the Portuguese, one of the reasons why many of the natives rejected Christianity.

The Spice Islands

In 1545, weary and feeling the need for a time of deep prayer in order to discern his next steps, Francis went to the ancient town of Mylapore on the eastern coast of India. After four months of intense prayer, he decided to leave his work in India in the hands of several fellow Jesuits as he went to pioneer the faith in the Spice Islands in Malaysia. From early 1546 to 1547, he labored—often by himself—among the island natives, traveling through thick jungles, even to places where the people were reported to be cannibalistic.

In Malacca, Francis met Anjiro, a samurai from Japan who had heard of the holy Father and sought him out. For his part, Francis became fascinated with the stories of Anjiro's homeland, which had only been opened up to the Western world a few years before. Francis was enchanted with this new land of culture and refinement, a land yet untainted by European corruption.

Japan

Francis landed on the southern tip of Japan on the Feast of the Assumption, 1549, together with Anjiro and two Spanish Jesuits. The local ruler (*daimyo*) gave them permission to preach, but the harvest was small. The Buddhist priests asked many questions, but few seemed persuaded by Francis' Japanese recitation of the basic truths of the faith.

In the autumn of 1550, Francis and his friends were given permission to go to Kyoto, the ancient capital, to meet with the emperor. Their journey is described in a letter by one of the Spanish priests who had stayed behind with some newly baptized Christians:

> They left here just as the *Yamassee*—the wind from the eastern mountains—began to blow, and when the first frosts and snows of this cold land began. But you know

> Father Francis! Such is the fire of the love of God within him that neither snows nor frosts nor fears nor dangers can deter him from spreading the gospel. . . . In the deep snow their sandals soon became useless and fell away, so that their bleeding feet made bloody tracks in the snow. And the crowds of boys and a rowdy rabble followed them, mimicking their speech, calling them names, and pelting them with stones and filth. With all this they never ceased preaching and confessing our holy faith.

The harrowing trip to Kyoto ended in disappointment. The Emperor held no power; it was the local *daimyos* who were the key to spreading the faith. Francis realized that his tattered clothing and simple lifestyle were a hindrance, so he went to Yamaguchi in new robes, bearing expensive gifts for the local rulers. A steady stream of converts came to them, and soon 500 people were baptized.

At the end of the summer of 1551, Francis received word that he was urgently needed in India. On the voyage back, a small sloop carrying some of the men was swept away by the violent sea. Francis went to his cabin and prayed for the return of the men. When the boat showed up at sundown, the men said they would have been lost had not Francis come to rescue them. Two Muslims who had been in the sloop were baptized as a result of that incident.

At the Mouth of the Canton River

The ship stopped at an island about six miles off the Chinese coast, and a sea captain talked about the wonders of

China. The captain had surreptitiously ventured inland—a forbidden practice that could expose foreigners to torture and death. Francis knew that Japan looked to China as its model in everything. If China accepted the faith, surely Japan would follow. The idea was hatched. Francis would find a way—however dangerous—to bring the Good News to China.

Francis hoped to be accompanied to China by his Portuguese friend and merchant, Diego Pereira, who was to be the Portuguese ambassador to China. However this plan never came to fruition. Francis and a Chinese boy from Goa then planned to rendezvous with a Chinese trader who could smuggle them into the country. They waited for him on Sancian, an island at the mouth of the Canton River.

On November 21, 1552, while still waiting, Francis came down with a fever. For ten days, Francis became weaker and weaker, speaking in his native Basque and frequently murmuring the name of Jesus in his delirium. At dawn on December 2, this adventurous missionary for Christ took his last breath in a small hut on the windy, nearly deserted island. It was the final death in a life full of daily acts of dying to self. Francis himself had observed years before, "What happiness equals that of dying a little every day, breaking our wills to seek and find not what is ours but that which is Christ's."

Francis never read a letter from Ignatius recalling him to Europe. As he had predicted, the two were never to see each other again in this life. In 1622, however, their lives were celebrated by the church: On the same day, they were both declared saints.

The Heavenly Pilgrim

Francis Xavier wrote this letter to
Ignatius of Loyola after arriving in Cape Comorin,
the southern tip of India, in 1544.

To the Reverend Father Ignatius, General of the Society, at Rome:

May the grace and charity of Our Lord always help and favor us, Amen. I set out with three native students at Goa seminary, and, on arrival here, we visited some villages the inhabitants of which, eight years ago, received baptism. As no Portuguese reside in this region, which is very sterile and poor, the faithful, without priests, know nothing more than that they were baptized. Since we came, I have been busy baptizing all infants born since then; some of these are so young as not to know left hand from right; others, the older ones, give me no peace begging me to teach them some prayer. They give me no time to say my office, nor yet to eat; such importunity has made me realize the meaning of the words "of such is the kingdom of God.". . .

I have received only one letter from you, dated February 1542. God alone knows the joy it gave me. It arrived here only two months ago, some twenty months after you had penned it! . . .

Such numbers become Christians that often my hands are numb at the end of a day from the fatigue of baptizing. And sometimes I lose my voice from the constant repetition of the Creed and other prayers and instruction. . . .

How many, in these countries, fail to become Christians, simply for the lack of a teacher of the Christian faith! Often

I think of running throughout the universities of Europe, and principally Paris and the Sorbonne, there to shout at the top of my voice, like one who had lost his senses—to tell those men whose learning is greater than their wish to put their knowledge to good use, how many souls, through their negligence, must lose Heaven and end up in hell. If all who, with so much labor, study letters, would pause to consider the account they must one day render God concerning the talents entrusted to them, I am sure that they would come to say: "Here I am, Lord. Send me where thou pleasest, even to India." How much happier and safer they would be, eventually, when facing that dreadful hour from which no man can escape. Then, with the faithful servant of the Gospel they could say: "Lord, five talents thou gavest me; behold five others I have gained . . ."

Pray that God who has separated us for the good of Christianity will one day reunite us in Heaven. For this intention invoke the prayers of those babes whom I baptized with my own hands in this land and whom God saw fit to call to his eternal mansions before they lost the robe of innocence with which I was privileged to clothe their souls. There must be, as I reckon, at least a thousand of them now; I often pray to these little saints to ask God that we, while exiled in this life, may know his will and accomplish it completely and in the manner that he desires.

At Cochin, January 1544.

Your most affectionate brother in Jesus Christ,
Francisco

The Life of Francis Xavier

1506 - Born in Navarre, the youngest of six children, to a noble Basque family

1512–1525 - Francis' father and brothers enter Navarre's fight against Spain to remain independent

1525 - Francis leaves home to study at the University of Paris

1527 - Meets Ignatius of Loyola

1532 - Receives Master of Arts degree and becomes lecturer

1534 - Francis, Ignatius, and five other men make vows in Montmartre on Aug. 15

1536 - Leaves Paris for Italy

1537 - Is ordained in Jun.

1540 - Leaves Italy for Portugal to prepare for journey to India

1541 - Sails for India on Apr. 17

1542 - Arrives in Goa after year-long journey

1542 - Arrives in Cape Comorin to work with pearl fishers

1546–1547 - Undertakes missionary journeys in Spice Islands in Malaysia; meets Anjiro in Malacca

1549–1551 - Makes first Christian converts in Japan

1552 - Arrives on Sancian, an island off the Chinese coast; dies from fever on Dec. 2

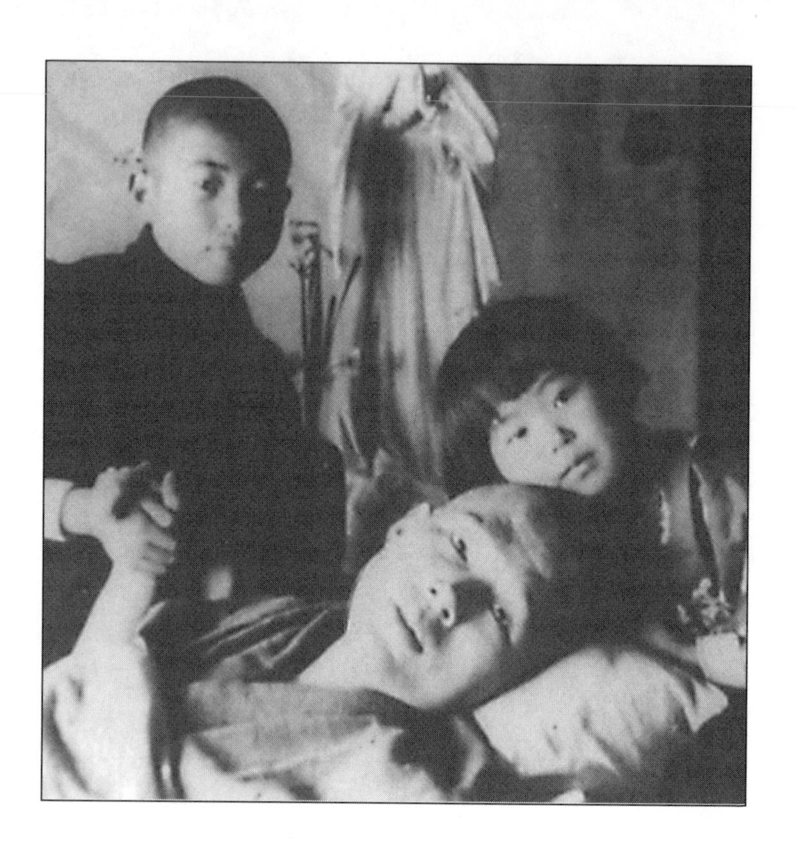

Blessed Are Those Who Mourn

Takashi Nagai

1908 - 1951

Takashi Nagai was born in 1908, into a family steeped in the traditions of ancient Japan and imbued with the spirit of Shinto—a sense of wonder at the natural world and a deep reverence for the spiritual world. His ancestors were of noble Samurai stock, and his grandfather was greatly revered for his artistic practice of herbal medicine. His birthplace, Shimane Prefecture, lies along the north coast of Honshu on the Sea of Japan. With its windswept valleys, deep green landscapes, and thatched-roof houses, it represents everything noble and timeless about Japan.

Everyone assumed that young Takashi would naturally follow the ancient way of the *Bushido*, the Samurai code of his ancestors. None of those who joined his parents in giving thanks before the ancestral gods for the birth of a son would have dreamed that Takashi would one day embrace both

Christianity and the atomic age. No one would have dreamed that he would become a living symbol of the gospel's command to love one's neighbor as oneself. He was just a red-faced, bawling infant with a large head and proud, curious eyes.

A Man without Moorings

Takashi grew up in a time when Japan was opening up to the West, thus his education was a mixture of *nihon-teki* ("very Japanese") reverence for nature and European rationalism. No one was offended when he decided to study Western medicine at the University of Nagasaki. Nor was he shocked when one of his professors, at the beginning of the semester, unveiled a cadaver before the class and announced, "Gentlemen, this is man, the object of our studies. A body with physical properties. Things you can see, weigh, test, measure. And this is all man is." Shintoism was out, atheism was in, and young Takashi was thrilled with the possibilities.

Takashi's philosophies were shattered, however, by the death of his mother in 1930. As he knelt at her bedside and watched her passing, he instinctively knew that she would not merely perish. "I who was so sure that there was no such thing as a spirit was now told otherwise; and I could not but believe! My mother's eyes told me that the human spirit lives on after death."

He sought answers in the writings of the French philosopher-scientist Blaise Pascal. Pascal's love for poetry and nature were indeed *nihon-teki*, but his statements of the limitations of the human mind repelled the youthful Japanese. This great mathematician insisted that the highest truths could not be grasped solely by the intellect, but by the heart reaching out to God in prayer.

Curious but cautious, when he returned to Nagasaki after his mother's funeral, Nagai decided to board with a Christian family in the city's northern district (Urakami), close by the university's hospital. He found an opening in the home of Sadakichi Moriyama and his wife, a Catholic couple in their fifties. He did not know that the Moriyamas' ancestors had been leaders of Nagasaki's "hidden Christians" who, from the late sixteenth to the late nineteenth centuries, had lived out the gospel in an illegal underground community, braving the ever-present danger of persecution, torture, and death for the sake of their faith in Christ.

The Moriyamas' deep reverence for God touched him, and he was intrigued by the fact that their acceptance of the gospel did not mean a rejection of everything Japanese. The Moriyamas were not traitors. In fact, they were more *nihon-teki* than many of the atheistic professors and students he knew!

Nagai received his qualifying degree in 1932 and took a post at the university in the new department of radiology, a poorly-funded, highly experimental, and potentially dangerous branch of research. Here, on the cutting edge of science, he could test the power and scope of his scientific atheism and still be free to continue investigating Christianity.

An Internal and External War

A year later, Nagai was drafted as an army surgeon and sent to the Manchurian front, where the realities of war eroded his idealism. He found it increasingly difficult to explain to soldiers why he had to amputate, or how they could live without sight or hearing. He vividly recalled one soldier who had been rendered blind and deaf by an exploding shell. The young man believed he had been captured by the Chinese and, in fear of torture, kept begging for death. How could science ever prevail over such primal reactions?

Not long after he arrived at the front, Midori, the Moriyamas' daughter, sent him a catechism. This strong, prayerful granddaughter of martyrs attracted him, and so he decided to read the book. When he came to the Ten Commandments, something happened inside of him. "I suddenly felt dirty. If there was a God and if there was a devil, I had spent my life observing the devil's ten commandments—pride, lust, covetousness, gluttony, anger. . . . I had done everything the book said was wrong." He also realized he was falling in love with Midori.

Nagai returned to Nagasaki confused and empty. After an abortive attempt to tell Midori of his growing love for her, he sought sanctuary in the cathedral. There, he met an aging priest whose parents and grandparents—like the Moriyamas—had endured torture and persecution for their faith. Nagai poured out his heart to him, and the priest repeated the urgings of Pascal and the catechism: To understand God, you must experience him, and you can only experience him by going down on your knees in prayer.

When he wasn't throwing himself into teaching and research, Nagai devoured scripture, attended Mass at the cathedral, and prayed quietly in his room. By June of 1934, Takashi understood the difference between the kingdom of God and the dominion of darkness. He knew that he was in darkness and needed the light of Christ. In the dimly-lit baptistery of Urakami Cathedral, in the presence of his priest friend, Takashi Nagai renounced sin and Satan, accepted Jesus into his heart, and was baptized into the church. Soon after, he and Midori were married.

The Power of the Atom

Nagai continued his radiation research, eventually becoming a pioneer in X-ray diagnosis. Thousands of patients came to him each year for treatment. With each diagnosis, experiment, or class demonstration, he exposed himself to dangerously high doses of gamma radiation. By the spring of 1945, he began noticing how difficult it was becoming for him to climb a flight of stairs, how tired he felt in the middle of the afternoon. Eventually, a colleague persuaded *him* to be X-rayed, and the results confirmed his fears—advanced leukemia, only a few years left to live, then a slow and painful death.

Takashi knew that the only way to face such frightening realities was through prayer. When he learned of his illness, his first reaction was to kneel and tell the Lord how hard it seemed and to ask him for the strength to understand and accept his plan. When he told Midori, she knelt before the family altar and prayed quietly. After a long moment, she told her husband, "We said before we were married that if our lives were spent for the glory of God, then life and death are beautiful. You have given everything you had for a very important work. It was for his glory."

To the best of his ability, Nagai continued his work, determined not to give in to illness or self-pity. He also monitored the international scene closely. Japan bombed Pearl Harbor in December 1941, bringing the United States into World

War II. Nagasaki University's hospital was opened to treat wounded soldiers. Eventually, the city was being subjected to almost daily air raids as Allied forces gradually moved closer to the island of Japan. It was only a matter of time, many thought, before enemy ground forces would land on Japan's mainland.

The Day of Darkness and Wind

On Wednesday morning, August 8, 1945, Nagai left home for the university as usual. He wouldn't be back until the evening of the next day because he was serving on air-raid duty that night. On Thursday morning, some friends invited Midori to accompany them on a walk into the countryside, but she declined. She was going to bring lunch to Takashi at the hospital. At around 11:00 a.m. on the morning of August 9, Nagai was in his office preparing a class lecture. The next few hours were stamped into his memory:

> There was a flash of blinding light. I thought: A bomb has fallen right at the university entrance! I intended to throw myself to the floor immediately, but before I could, window-pane glass rushed in with a frightening noise. A giant hand seemed to grab me and hurl me three meters. Fragments of glass flew about like leaves in a whirlwind. My eyes were open and I had a glimpse of the outside—planks, beams, clothing were doing a weird dance in the air. All the objects in my room had joined in, and I felt the end had come. My right side was cut by glass, and warm blood coursed down my cheek and neck.

> The giant invisible fist had gone berserk and was smashing everything in the office. Various objects fell on top of me while I listened to strange noises like mountains rumbling back and forth. Then came pitch darkness as if the ferro-concrete hospital were an express train that had just rushed headlong into a tunnel. . . . Panic gripped my heart when I heard crackling flames and sniffed acrid smoke. I was conscious of my sins, especially the ones I had intended to confess that very afternoon, and directed my whole attention to the Lord our Judge and asked his forgiveness.

Nagai was less than half a mile from the epicenter of the second atomic bomb dropped by Allied forces on Japan. Hiroshima had been devastated a few days earlier. Nagai had survived only because his building, made of reinforced concrete, was able to withstand the force of the initial blast, and he was in the far end of the building. When freed from his room, he found that only a handful of his staff were still alive. The devastation horrified him. Bloated, skinless corpses were strewn about the ground in awkward positions. Bodies hung upside down in stone walls and fences, headless or limbless. Fires had broken out everywhere, and some of the few who survived were crawling or stumbling toward him, croaking, "Water, water. I'm burning up!"

With a small band of doctors and nurses, Nagai labored all day, treating the wounded and encouraging his colleagues. But his own wounds and sickness soon took their toll, and sometime that evening he collapsed into unconsciousness. The next day, however, he awoke and continued his work with the hundreds of survivors from Urakami who had made their way to the hospital seeking help. Throughout this ordeal, when he wasn't giving orders or comforting a patient, Nagai took up the Japanese tradition of the *Nembutsu*—a short verse repeated over and over. But instead of quoting Confucius, Takashi Nagai, the Japanese Christian, prayed the scriptures, "The heavens and the earth will pass away, but my words will never vanish."

A couple of days later, at his first opportunity, an exhausted Nagai walked to the site of his home and found his beloved Midori's charred bones amidst the wreckage that was once their kitchen. Kneeling beside her, he discovered a melted blob that had been her rosary, lying next to her right hand. Even as he wept, he was filled with gratitude that his wife had died praying.

The Sacrificial Lamb and the Beatitudes

Rather than begin a new life with his children in another city, Nagai decided to remain in Nagasaki and live among the ruins. With the help of some friends, he built a makeshift hut on the site of his old house and with only the barest of essentials, he and his two children (Makoto and Kayano) moved back home. The hut was only about seven feet by ten feet, constructed of charred beams, heat-warped tin, and a thin mat. There, Nagai spent most of his time teaching his children and asking God to help him understand what had happened to him and to the city.

Many other residents followed Nagai's example and returned home. Urakami had become a jumble of rubble, ash, and sorry-looking huts. Many drew strength from Nagai's faith and deliberate simplicity. He dedicated himself to prayer, seeking God's wisdom and learning to remain in the divine presence all day, even as he wrote articles, spoke with visitors, or taught his children. He had always loved the Beatitudes; now, more than ever, he pondered them, asking the Lord to write them on his heart.

The Catholic bishop of Nagasaki determined to hold an open-air requiem Mass on the grounds of the burnt-out cathedral, and he asked Nagai to speak to the Christian survivors. Nagai accepted, and on November 29, 1945, he stood before thousands of fellow believers, all of whom had lost so much. In a quiet, compelling voice, he explained that the eight thousand Christians who had died instantly in the bomb were specially chosen by God. They were a holocaust, an expiation for all the sins committed during the war. These dead were unblemished lambs, sacrificial offerings to the Father in union with Christ, the one perfect Lamb of God.

Those who survived—himself as well as his audience—were alive only because they were not worthy to offer so pure a sacrifice. They had not purified themselves enough to be acceptable, as their fallen brothers and sisters had been, to be completely united with Christ in his death and resurrection. For the survivors, the only way lay in the Beatitudes—poverty of spirit, hunger and thirst for righteousness, meekness, and mercy. Above all, "Blessed are those who mourn, for they will be comforted." Nagai concluded, "Let us give thanks that Nagasaki was chosen for the sacrifice. Let us give thanks that through this sacrifice peace was given to the world and freedom of religion to Japan. May the souls of the faithful departed, through the mercy of God, rest in peace. Amen."

Pray! Please Pray!

Nagai spent the rest of his life bedridden in a smaller but better-constructed hut built next to the one inhabited by his children, his mother-in-law, and his brother's family. He named this new hut, *Nyokodo*, "Love-your-neighbor-as-yourself-home." He wrote extensively, and his books and articles—both spiritual and scientific—received wide acceptance. *Nyokodo* became a focal point in Nagasaki for pilgrims and citizens alike. Nagai treated all who came to see him with equal respect and honor, speaking of the love of Christ and encouraging them to forgive, to love one another, and to pray for peace.

Even as he became increasingly popular, Nagai insisted all the more firmly on his deep need for Christ and that any good that people might see in him was only Christ in him. Takashi Nagai, he often said, was a selfish, foolish man whom Jesus loved, forgave, and gave new life. He never tired of sharing with his thousands of visitors the simple words of Pascal, "You can only find the answer on your knees. Pray and believe, and God will give you peace."

On May 1, 1951, Takashi Nagai passed from earth to heaven. After a particularly painful night, he asked to be carried to the hospital so that his colleagues and students could observe first hand the final effects of radiation poisoning. After a brief stop at the newly erected cathedral to pray for peace, he was taken to a hospital room and solemnly bathed in preparation for his passing, a Japanese tradition. Everyone expected him to die slowly, but he surprised them. His son, Makoto, was holding the family crucifix over his bed, and in a remarkable surge of strength, Nagai's left arm shot up and grasped the cross. In a firm voice, he called out, "Pray! Please pray!" With that, he closed his eyes. More than 20,000 people attended his funeral, and throughout Japan, bells were rung in his memory—in Buddhist temples and Shinto shrines as well as in Christian churches.

Takashi Nagai had lived through one of the twentieth century's most terrifying moments to stand as a witness to the transforming power of the gospel. His influence is still felt in Nagasaki's annual commemoration of "that day" in 1945. Every year, on August 6, throngs of people converge on Hiroshima and hold political demonstrations and rallies, many of them characterized by noisy anti-West slogans. Three days later, another group of people gather in Nagasaki to pray for reconciliation and peace. Many Japanese say, "Hiroshima is anger, Nagasaki is prayer." This is the legacy of a once proud atheist who, through faith and trust, embodied the poverty of spirit and inner strength of Jesus Christ, the unblemished Lamb of God.

This is a portion of Takashi Nagai's funeral address for the victims of the atomic bomb, delivered on November 29, 1945.

Is there not a profound relationship between the destruction of Nagasaki and the end of the war? Nagasaki, the only holy place in all Japan—was it not chosen as a victim, a pure lamb, to be slaughtered and burned on the altar of sacrifice to expiate the sins committed by humanity in the Second World War?

The human family has inherited the sin of Adam who ate the fruit of the forbidden tree; we have inherited the sin of Cain who killed his younger brother; we have forgotten that we are children of God; we have believed in idols; we have disobeyed the law of love. Joyfully we have hated one another; joyfully we have killed one another. And now at last we have brought this great and evil war to an end. But in order to restore peace to the world it was not sufficient to repent. We had to obtain God's pardon through the offering of a great sacrifice. . . .

Our church of Nagasaki kept the faith during four hundred years of persecution when religion was proscribed and the blood of martyrs flowed freely. During the war this same church never ceased to pray day and night for a lasting peace. Was it not, then, the one unblemished lamb that had to be offered on the altar of God? Thanks to the sacrifice of this lamb many millions who would otherwise have fallen victim to the ravages of war have been saved.

How noble, how splendid was that holocaust of August 9, when flames soared up from the cathedral, dispelling the darkness of war and bringing the light of peace! In the very depth of our grief we reverently saw here something beautiful, something pure, something sublime. Eight thousand people, together with their priests, burning with pure smoke, entered into eternal life. All without exception were good people whom we deeply mourn.

How happy are those people who left this world without knowing the defeat of their country! How happy are the pure lambs who rest in the bosom of God! Compared with them how miserable is the fate of us who have survived! Japan is conquered. Urakami is totally destroyed. A waste of ash and rubble lies before our eyes. We have no houses, no food, no clothes. Our fields are devastated. Only a remnant has survived. In the midst of the ruins we stand in groups of two or three looking blankly at the sky.

Why did we not die with them on that day, at that time, in this house of God? Why must we alone continue this miserable existence?

It is because we are sinners. Ah! Now indeed we are forced to see the enormity of our sins! It is because I have not made expiation for my sins that I am left behind. Those are left who were so deeply rooted in sin that they were not worthy to be offered to God. . . .

"Blessed are those that mourn for they shall be comforted." We must walk this way of expiation faithfully and sincerely. And as we walk in hunger and thirst, ridiculed, penalized, scourged, pouring with sweat and covered with blood, let us remember how Jesus Christ carried his cross to the hill of Calvary. He will give us courage.

The Life of Takashi Nagai

1908 - Born in Shimane Prefecture, Japan

1920 - Boards with relatives in Matsue to attend secondary school

1928 - Enters University of Nagasaki

1930 - His mother dies

1931 - Boards with Sadakichi Moriyama and family

1932 - Takes post in Nagasaki University's radiology department

1933 - Drafted into army as surgeon and goes to Manchuria

1934 - Returns to Japan, becomes a Catholic, and marries Midori Moriyama

Spring 1945 - Discovers he has advanced leukemia

Aug. 9, 1945 - Survives the atom bomb explosion, but Midori dies

1946 - Writes *The Bells of Nagasaki*, which is published in 1949 and becomes a best seller

1951 - Dies on May 1

Catholic News Service

In the Shadow of the Cross

Blessed Edith Stein

1891 - 1942

The place: Westerbork, a Nazi detention camp in the north of Holland. The time: August 4, 1942—high water mark of the Third Reich and the Nazis' attempts to destroy all Jews. More than a hundred thousand men, women, and children passed through this camp on their way to other concentration camps in eastern Germany and Poland. Once they reached their final destination—Auschwitz, Buchenwald, or somewhere else, they would die. Many sensed what was awaiting them, even though the details were vague, and they were assailed by oppression, confusion, and terror.

A survivor of this camp, Julius Marcan of Cologne, later testified:

> There was a spirit of indescribable misery in the camp; the new prisoners, especially, suffered from extreme

> anxiety. Edith Stein went among the women like an angel, comforting, helping and consoling them. Many of the mothers . . . had sat moaning for days, not giving any thought to their children. Edith Stein immediately set about taking care of these little ones. She washed them, combed their hair, and tried to make sure they were fed and cared for.

In this environment, Edith Stein, a highly respected Jewish-born philosopher and teacher, and now a prisoner of the Nazis, moved "like an angel." Even though she perceived more clearly than many others the depth of suffering that her people endured, in the midst of this awareness she offered comfort and peace. She had shone, in one of the darkest moments in the history of Abraham's descendants. And while Edith herself joined the millions of others who were to perish in Nazi gas chambers, her witness stands out because she somehow overcame death before it visited her.

Promising Beginnings

Edith Hedwig Stein was born in Germany, on October 12, 1891, the feast of Yom Kippur, the Jewish Day of Atonement. She was the seventh child of a devout Jewish couple for whom the observances and feasts of their people were the embodiment of their faith. From very early on, the driving force in this large family was the mother, Auguste Stein, a woman of great endurance and deep devotion. Strict in discipline, Frau Stein planted deep within her children a sincere charity and an abhorrence of sin: No matter how difficult things were, they always gave to the poor.

When Edith was only two years old, her father died suddenly. Rather than give in to grief and sell her husband's lumber company, Auguste accepted God's provision, shouldered the work herself, and made the company a success. When she was young, Edith faithfully accompanied her mother to the synagogue every week, but she eventually abandoned the faith of her parents. In her studies at school, she excelled both by talent and sheer force of will. Prodded by a tireless intellect, she hungered for firm, reliable truth and could no longer accept the religion of her childhood, which didn't answer the questions challenging her intellect. She needed something more and, until she found it, belief was impossible.

Graduating from secondary school in 1911 with high honors, Edith was accepted by the university at Breslau. She began studying education, changed to psychology, and later took up philosophy. Questions haunted her day and night, often robbing her of sleep. The answers she sought tended to be elusive, the questions too profound. Finally, she saw some hope in philosophy, which she aggressively pursued and at which she excelled.

Edith studied under Professor Edmund Husserl, one of the most influential philosophers of the early twentieth century. Husserl played a key role in the formation of a number of later philosophers, including Jean-Paul Sartre. Central to his approach was a detailed search for a stable foundation for life in this world. Edith showed such promise under Husserl that she eventually became one of his most favored assistants. She also gained recognition in her own right as a gifted teacher and writer.

A Breakthrough

In 1917, Edith received news that Adolf Reinach, a professor whom she deeply respected and admired, had died in the Battle of Flanders. Not long after the start of World War I, both Reinach and his wife had become Christians and had been baptized into the Lutheran Church. Edith was asked to help put his papers and writings in order. The prospect intimidated her. What words of comfort could she offer his widow? She was painfully aware of her own inner questions, her lack of answers; the task seemed beyond her. It was only out of love for her friends that she agreed to do it.

To Edith's amazement, she didn't find a widow overwhelmed by grief, angry, or embittered by her husband's tragic death. Instead, she found a woman of hope, herself consoling grieving friends. That encounter touched something within Edith. All her logical seeking, all her philosophical training, had not prepared her for the experience. Recalling the incident years later, she wrote:

> It was my first encounter with the Cross. For the first time, I was seeing with my very eyes the church, born from its Redeemer's sufferings, triumphant over the sting of death. That was the moment my unbelief collapsed and Christ shone forth—in the mystery of the Cross.

Edith knew that she must examine this phenomenon with the same vigor and thoroughness that she had given her previous studies. The reality of Christ confronted her, and she could not ignore him. She began to read the New Testament.

From Light to Life

The answers did not come quickly. Edith sensed that she was coming to faith, but the final step seemed too difficult for her to take. Around this time, she wrote:

> A convicted atheist learns through personal experience that there actually is a God. . . . Yet he can still refuse to ground himself in it or to let it become effective in him. Or, again, someone can offer me affection. There's no way I can stop him from doing it, but I don't have to respond to it. I can always pull myself away.

God's light had dawned upon her, but she had yet to decide to allow the light to become life for her. Edith saw the question that all Christians must answer: Is Christianity a matter of light, a "feeling" of God, or is it a matter of life, a decision to be formed by God and not by desires or achievements—great though they may be? The cross stood at the center of this question, and Edith could not ignore it.

During the summer of 1921 Edith spent some time at a friend's farm. One evening, her hosts went out, leaving Edith alone. Browsing through their library, she happened upon the autobiography of St. Teresa of Avila, the great Spanish Catholic reformer of the sixteenth century. She sat down to read it. Teresa's experience of difficult questions and elusive answers was so similar to hers that Edith could not stop reading.

Teresa had learned to put aside her mind's questions and objections and open her heart to the love of God in Christ. The mystery of God's love could not be deduced from logical investigation. The seeming folly, but apparent love, of a crucified savior had impressed itself in Teresa's heart, and she surrendered to God in faith, no longer seeking him through analysis.

Edith read throughout the night and on into the morning, and when she finished, she could only respond, "This is the truth." Finally, the philosopher had found her answers. The very next day, she bought a catechism and a missal and began to study them thoroughly, and on January 1, 1922, she was baptized into the Catholic Church.

From the moment of her conversion, Edith deeply desired to follow in Teresa's footsteps. Like Teresa, who had been a Carmelite nun, she yearned to embrace a life of poverty, chastity, and reverent submission within a community of similarly committed Christians. For Edith, this meant joining the Carmelite order. Her dream had to be deferred for ten years, however, out of consideration for her mother and because of her growing prominence in Germany as a Catholic woman philosopher.

Closed and Opened Doors

Edith took a teaching position at a Benedictine convent school in Speyer. For eight years, she lived in her own simple room in the convent, observing private vows and sharing in the life of the Benedictine sisters. Her composure never seemed to change from the intense, quiet, stable woman of God she had become. She had high expectations and a compelling ability to show compassion and concern. Consequently, students and sisters alike were greatly attracted to her. She was also prayerful and would kneel before the Blessed Sacrament for hours at a time, lost in contemplation and love for the Messiah.

While in Speyer, Edith continued to contribute to scholarly journals and give lectures, both in Germany and throughout Western Europe. She became increasingly known and respected in academic circles. Requests for lectures poured in from everywhere and, in 1930, she decided it was time to leave Speyer and devote herself fully to academic work.

Returning to her mother's home, she applied for university professorships and continued to write and lecture. But the atmosphere in Germany was beginning to change as the National Socialist Party (Nazis) gained popularity and power. Because she was a woman and a Jew, no university would take her. She accepted this calmly and instead took a post at the Catholic Educational Institute in Münster in 1932.

In 1933, Hitler became chancellor of Germany and official restrictions against the Jews began. Edith was informed that she could no longer teach at Münster. Ironically, she was grateful: She had become less useful to the outside world, and the way opened up for her to enter the monastery. Her only real difficulty was the reaction of her eighy-four-year-old mother.

For Frau Stein, Edith's decision meant more than losing her beloved daughter. It was a betrayal of everything Edith had become—of everything she had trained Edith to be. How could an independent, strong-willed woman, a success in the world, and most importantly, a chosen daughter of Israel, take such a step? On learning of Edith's intended commitment to Christ as a Carmelite nun, the aged woman wept bitterly. She could only respond in disbelief, "Why did you have to get to know him? He was a good man—I'm not saying anything against him. But why did he have to go and make himself God?"

Blessed by the Cross

Edith entered the Carmelite monastery at Cologne in October 1933, at the age of forty-two. She expected the transition to be difficult for an academic woman in her middle years, but she felt perfectly content. With characteristic intensity, she threw herself into monastic life. Even household duties—which were so unfamiliar to her—became opportunities to grow in humility and love. Her efforts, sometimes awkward, endeared her all the more to her new sisters.

When she made her simple profession of vows, Edith took the name Teresa Benedicta of the Cross. She chose "Teresa" because of her debt to Teresa of Avila. "Benedicta" (which means "blessed") reflects the Benedictine nuns with whom she lived for eight years. Finally, by adding "the Cross," her name could also read, "Teresa, Blessed by the Cross." The cross had been at the turning point of Edith's life—when she encountered a young widow's victory over death—and it remained central to her life with Christ.

The depth to which Edith identified herself with the cross shows itself in her reaction to the increased persecution that her people, the Jews, were enduring at the hands of the Nazis:

> I spoke with the Savior to tell him that I realized it was his Cross that was now being laid upon the Jewish people, that the few who had understood this had the responsibility of carrying it in the name of all, and that I myself was willing to do this, if he would only show me how.

Union with the Crucified

As time progressed, Edith learned how she would indeed be true to her name and carry the Savior's cross. On the night of November 9, 1938, the S.S. mounted a full-scale attack on Jewish homes, synagogues, and businesses throughout Germany, shattering windows, assaulting Jews, and destroying property. Deportations to labor camps increased at a horrifying rate, and Jews desperately tried to flee Germany.

Edith knew she could not remain in Cologne; she would be placing all the sisters in her convent in grave danger. Consequently, on December 31, 1938, under cover of night, she crossed into Holland and was received at the Carmelite monastery in Echt. About a year later, she was joined by her sister Rosa, who had also embraced Christ and become a Catholic.

In 1940, the Nazis overran Holland and began deporting the Jews there as well. Edith's Catholicism offered her some protection, but only for a time. By early 1942, she and Rosa were summoned frequently to Nazi headquarters and were subjected to long, intimidating interrogations. On July 26, a letter from the Bishop of Utrecht (Holland), in which he spoke out against the Nazi occupying forces and the deportation of Jews, was read in all Catholic churches in Holland.

On August 2, in retaliation for the Bishop's letter, all Catholics with Jewish background in Holland were arrested. Later that afternoon, two officers arrived at the monastery and gave Edith and Rosa five minutes to gather their necessities. As they were being taken to a waiting car, Rosa began to get anxious and disoriented. Taking her hand, Edith said calmly, "Come, Rosa. We are going for our people."

The next seven days they spent in holding camps and packed railway cars. Many people gave in to fear and depression, but Edith remained calm. As she observed the depth of her people's sufferings and began to experience these sufferings herself, a change came over her. Some say she looked as if she were bearing a great pain in her heart—but never for herself, only for the people around her. Finally, on August 9, 1942, Edith and Rosa, accompanied by thousands of their fellow Jews, arrived at Auschwitz where, most likely on that same day, they were executed in a gas chamber.

Hail to Thee, O Cross!

On January 25, 1987, Pope John Paul II beatified Edith Stein as a martyr of the Holocaust, and on October 11, 1998, she will be canonized in Rome. While she was only one of several million Christians who died in Nazi concentration camps, the way in which Edith faced death offered a distinct testimony to the transforming power of the cross of Christ. Every martyr, in one way or another, lives out Jesus' own self-description, "I am the good shepherd. The good shepherd lays down his life for the sheep. . . . No one takes it from me, but I lay it down of my own accord" (John 10:11, 18).

Edith willingly laid down her life of her own accord—long before she passed through the gates of Auschwitz. From the time of her baptism, this intelligent and independent woman sought to live simply and to submit her ways to the will of Christ. Her submission was manifested in her delaying entry into religious life for ten years, in her firm dedication to a life of prayer, and in joining the monastery itself, where she left behind the acclaimed, self-possessed woman of the academic world that she had become.

By the power of the cross, Edith could deny a life based on desires that clouded her vision of Christ crucified. By the power of the same cross, the Spirit enabled her to offer her life for her people, praying in reparation and atonement for all of those who suffered as she would suffer one day.

Perhaps the most striking witness to Edith's "martyrdom-before-death" is her last testament, which she composed at the monastery in Echt in 1939:

> I joyfully accept in advance the death God has appointed me, in perfect submission to his most holy will. May the Lord accept my life and death for the honor and glory of his name, for the needs of his holy Church . . . for the Jewish people, that the Lord may be received by his own and his kingdom come in glory, for the deliverance of Germany and peace throughout the world, and finally, for all my relatives living and dead and all whom God has given me: may none of them be lost.

"The Message of the Cross," taken from
The Science of the Cross, completed in 1942,
by Edith Stein.

The word of the cross is the gospel St. Paul preaches to Jews and Gentiles. He presents it as a simple testimony, without oratorical adornments and without attempting to convince his hearers by rational proofs. He draws all his strength from his subject. This is the cross of Christ, i.e. Christ's death on the cross and the crucified Christ himself. Christ is the strength of God and the wisdom of God, not only because he is sent by God, being the Son of God and himself God, but because he has been crucified. For his death on the cross is the means which God's unfathomable wisdom has devised to redeem us.

In order to show that the strength and wisdom of men cannot accomplish their redemption God gives us his redemptive power to him who appears weak and foolish by human standards; who desires to be nothing of himself but lets only God's power act in him, who has "emptied" himself and "become obedient" "even unto the death of the cross." The redemptive power raises to life those in whom the divine life had died through sin. This power has entered into the Word of the Cross, through which it penetrates to all who accept it without demanding signs or rational proof. In them it becomes that formative, life-giving power which we have called the Science of the Cross. . . .

But even now, "in the flesh," we have a share in it, because we have faith. We believe that Christ has died for us to give us life. This faith unites us to him as the members are united to their Head, opening our souls to receive his life. Thus living faith in Christ crucified and surrender to him give us life and are the beginning of future glory. Hence our only glory is the Cross: "God forbid that I should glory, save in the cross of our Lord Jesus Christ: by whom the world is crucified to me, and I to the world."

If a man has decided to follow Christ he is dead to the world and the world is dead to him. He bears the marks of the Lord in his body, is weak and despised by men, but for this very reason he is strong, because God's power is strong in the weak. Knowing this, the disciple of Jesus not only accepts the Cross that has been laid on him but crucifies himself: "They that are Christ's have crucified their flesh, with the vices and concupiscences." They have fought an unrelenting battle against their nature so that the life of sin should die in them and make room for the life of the spirit.

This is the point. The Cross is not an end in itself. It is raised up and points above itself. Nevertheless, it is not only a sign, it is the strong weapon of Christ, the shepherd's staff with which the divine David fights against the infernal Goliath, with which he knocks at the gate of heaven and opens it. Then the divine light streams out, embracing all those who follow the crucified Lord.

The Life of Edith Stein

1891 - Born on Oct. 12 in Germany to devout Jewish parents

1893 - Edith's father dies

1911 - Graduates with high honors from secondary school

1917 - Asked to assemble papers of her deceased professor; is struck by his widow's peace and trust in God

1921 - Encounters autobiography of St. Teresa of Avila and feels she has discovered truth

1922 - Is baptized into Catholic Church

1922-1930 - Teaches at Benedictine convent school in Speyer

1930 - Returns to mother's home; lectures and writes

1932 - Teaches at Catholic Educational Institute in Münster

1933 - Nazi restrictions against Jews force Edith to leave the school in Münster; she enters Carmelite monastery in Cologne in Oct.

1938 - Realizing she is placing her sisters in danger, Edith escapes into Holland and is received at the Carmelite monastery in Echt

1942 - Arrested on Aug. 2 by Nazis; transferred to Auschwitz on Aug. 9 and executed

Tercentenary painting of Saint Alphonsus by G. A. Lomuscio, courtesy of Liguori Publications

The Gentle Shepherd

Saint Alphonsus Liguori

1696 - 1787

An eighteenth-century European Catholic seeking to please the Lord might have had reason to despair. The prevailing theology of the day depicted God as a stern taskmaster who laid impossible burdens on his creatures. In this view, God expected blind obedience to a long list of rules. It was not uncommon for confessors to withhold absolution and to discourage people from receiving Communion too frequently. The law seemed to be everything, and individual human conscience had little, if any, say in determining the rightness of an action. A popular manual for confessors, noted one dissenting priest, breathed "fury, passion, sternness and fanaticism" and drove "the faithful to desperation."

Alphonsus Maria de Liguori, a Neapolitan nobleman, was formed in this strict "Rigorist" tradition, and it left an indelible mark on his character. Especially in his younger days, Liguori was scrupulous to a fault, always worried that he had somehow offended God. It is one of the ironies of church history that this lawyer-turned-priest revolutionized theology and pastoral practice with an approach that (according to the same priest quoted above) preached "charity, sweetness and moderation." Although scorned by leading theologians of his time, many of Alphonsus' works have become treasured Christian classics whose relevance endure to this day.

Why did his teachings strike such a chord? Most likely because they were rooted in his own experiences in prayer and as a pastor. As he grew closer to the Lord, Alphonsus came to see the futility of numerous rules. Keenly aware of God's love—most vividly expressed in the Passion—he sought to preach this love and to show how deeply God desires our love in return.

From Serving the Courts to Serving God

Born in 1696—the eldest of eight children—Alphonsus earned his law degree at just seventeen years of age. His father, a navy captain and strict authoritarian, was devout but had no plans for his eldest son—who was his heir—to enter the priesthood. However, on a retreat in 1722, Alphonsus experienced a deep encounter with the Lord and decided to make a private vow of celibacy, even as his father was arranging a marriage that would probably have been socially and financially advantageous for him.

It was also around this time that Alphonsus, ever the perfectionist, lost his first court case—an important one involving large sums of money and prominent Neapolitan noblemen. Walking out of the courtroom in disgust, he cried: "Ah, world, I know you now!" He went home and locked himself in his room for three days, during which time he ended his legal career. He chose to enter the priesthood instead.

Both as a seminarian and diocesan priest, Liguori threw himself into apostolic work, often laboring to the brink of exhaustion. He joined the Apostolic Missions, a group of priests who planned highly organized evangelistic programs that involved sermons, confessions, catechism, and prayer in the city of Naples. His simple preaching style became popular and attracted not only the uneducated, but the local nobility as well.

Alphonsus quickly discovered that the Rigorist approach bore little fruit in the confessional. Stressing instead God's mercy in the spirit of the prodigal son, he soon became a sought-after confessor. He and several companions reached out to the very poor living in inner-city neighborhoods—people known as the *lazzaroni*—to catechize them. Soon, a movement known as the "Evening Chapel" developed as groups of poor laypeople from all over the city met together to pray and learn about their faith.

The Way of Prayer

As Alphonsus moved away from the Rigorist school of theology, he began to see the importance of prayer in the ordinary flow of laypeople's lives. Prayer was the only way, he believed, that people could receive the grace they needed to overcome temptation. Strict adherence to rules could never take the place of a living relationship with God. Many of his pastoral writings emphasized this point, as he assured his readers that God gave everyone the ability to pray. In his preface to *The Great Means of Salvation*, published in 1759, for example, he wrote:

> I do not think I have written a more useful work than this one, in which I speak of prayer as a necessary and certain means of obtaining salvation and all the graces we need for it. If it were in my power, I would distribute a copy to every Catholic in the world to show him the absolute necessity of prayer for salvation.

In spite of his preaching about God's love and mercy, however, Alphonsus had to fight, throughout his lifetime, a tendency to be scrupulous. His solution was to pledge absolute obedience to his spiritual director, who could then relieve his constant anxiety that he had displeased God.

Life for the young priest was arduous. He worked so hard that he brought himself to the edge of collapse and was advised to take several weeks' rest. Traveling by sea, he and a few fellow priests were caught in a storm near the Amalfi Coast and decided to remain at a place just outside of the town of Scala for their vacation. They were soon visited by poor shepherds who were hungering for the gospel. In Naples, many men were ordained because it provided a way for the family property to escape taxation. As a consequence, there was an average of one priest for every hundred people. Here in the mountainous countryside, however, the people had no one to teach them about Christ. Liguori and his friends abandoned their vacation plans and launched a number of missions to serve these peasant families.

Launching a New Congregation

After returning to Naples, Alphonsus gave a retreat for a convent in Scala. During the retreat, one sister experienced a vision in which she felt the Lord calling her to establish a new religious community. Asked to pray about the vision's authenticity, Liguori discerned that God had indeed spoken and that he should help organize the new community. In 1731, the rule was adopted. Later that year, the same sister received another vision in which Jesus said he wanted Alphonsus to form a new congregation of men as well.

His friend, Father Thomas Falcoia, urged him to consider founding such an order, but Alphonsus was still a young priest and very committed to the missionary work he was then doing. Still, he couldn't let go of the idea and decided to go ahead with it. Several priests whose opinions he valued encouraged him, but his friends in Naples condemned the idea, calling him mentally unbalanced, arrogant, and under the influence of a deluded nun.

Despite initial setbacks and disputes, Liguori's community grew in numbers, and several houses were established. The men lived austerely, often without adequate food or clothing. Having refined the mission model he used in Naples, Alphonsus sent his priests into small towns and villages. They would give stirring sermons, hear confessions, and teach the people how to pray.

At the beginning of his priesthood, Alphonsus had vowed never to waste a moment that could be put to service for the

Lord—and it appears that he lived up to that vow. In addition to leading the congregation and conducting missions, he became a prolific writer of books and pastoral guides. Nine editions of his great work, *Moral Theology*, were published during his lifetime, along with more than a hundred other titles.

In his writings, Alphonsus emphasized the importance of forming an upright conscience so that people could use their God-given freedom to make proper moral decisions. For Liguori, a well-formed conscience could make God's laws come alive far more effectively than a long list of prohibitive and sometimes arbitrary rules. Even more importantly, a well-formed conscience would allow a person to respond to God creatively and out of love.

A Bishop of the Poor

By 1761, the sixty-five-year-old Alphonsus Liguori was in semi-retirement at the congregation's monastery in Pagani—partially deaf and blind, asthmatic, and suffering from a damaged leg that caused him to limp. Yet God was not ready to let him retire! In 1762, Pope Clement XIII appointed him Bishop of St. Agatha of the Goths, a diocese near Naples. The news put him into a deep depression, and he begged the Pope to change his mind—to no avail.

For thirteen years, until he was almost eighty years old, Alphonsus was a bishop of the poor. He chose a glass ring and a simple iron cross, and served his illustrious guests vegetable soup and a little boiled beef. With his characteristic zeal for pastoring, he sought to educate the local clergy and invited the priests from his own congregation to give missions. When famine struck in the winter of 1763, he borrowed money from friends to obtain grain and dried vegetables for his people. "The bishop must think of the poor who have no one to dry their tears. They are special members of Jesus Christ," he said, often forgoing his own meals because he was so painfully aware of those who had nothing to eat.

As his health continued to deteriorate, Liguori asked to be relieved of his duties, but was again refused. Finally, in April 1775, Pope Pius VI accepted his resignation, and he returned to Pagani to live out his final days. Yet Liguori lived for twelve more years, often in intense physical pain. A disease that had first settled in his right hip now traveled up and down his body, causing such a curvature in his neck that a deep wound formed where his chin pressed against his chest.

"I Have Been Betrayed!"

Probably more painful than his physical ailments, however, were the problems that cropped up within his congregation. Eight houses existed—four in the kingdom of Naples and four in the Papal States. The congregation had received papal approval in 1749 under the title of the Fathers of the Most Holy Redeemer, or the Redemptorists. But the rule still lacked a royal stamp of approval from the king of Naples—a necessary step to ensure its continued existence. Alphonsus sent two trusted advisers to the court at Naples to obtain approval, but in the negotiations, the rule became compromised almost beyond recognition. Worse still, the nearly blind Liguori signed the new rule in 1779 without fully knowing its contents. When he learned how the original rule had been changed, he sobbed in anguish, "I have been betrayed!"

Since the rule had been changed so drastically by the King, the four Naples houses risked papal dismissal from the original congregation. At the instigation of the leaders of the houses in the Papal States—who wanted to be independent from Naples—and before he had heard the Neapolitan side of the story, Pius VI signed a decree that essentially dismissed from the order Alphonsus and the members of the houses in Naples. Hearing the news, Alphonsus sank into a deep depression. "Do not call me founder," he told a fellow priest. "Call me a miserable sinner." In the last few months of his life, however, he found peace, and on August 1, 1787—no longer a member of the order he had founded—Alphonsus Liguori died.

Liguori was canonized in 1839, only fifty-two years after his death—the only professional moral theologian ever to be officially declared a saint by the church. His Redemptorist order has grown and spread to all parts of the world. In the 200 years since his death, more than 20,000 editions of his works have been published, making his writings second only to the Bible in popularity. In 1871, he was made a Doctor of the Church, and in 1950, he was named a patron of confessors and moral theologians.

The Gentle Shepherd

From *The Practice of the Love of Jesus Christ* by Alphonsus Liguori.

Those who love Jesus Christ hope for all things from him. Just as love believes all things, so love hopes all things.

Hope increases charity and charity increases hope, because hope in God's goodness undoubtedly helps us grow in love for Jesus Christ. Saint Thomas says that at the precise moment that we hope to receive something from a person we also begin to love that person. And this is why the Lord forbids us to place our complete trust in creatures; the more we trust in God the more we shall grow in his holy love.

How quickly we grow in holiness when our hearts are filled with confidence in God! We soar rather than run; for in making God the basis of all our hope, we put aside our own weakness and borrow the strength of God himself, which he shares with all those who trust in him.

Like the eagle that flies nearest the sun, those who trust in God gradually become detached from the earth and more and more united to God by love.

Just as hope increases the love of God, so love increases hope, because charity makes us the adopted children of God. By nature, we are creatures of God; but by grace we become children of God through the merits of Jesus Christ. And if charity makes us children of God, it also makes us heirs of heaven. Heirs are entitled to the father's estate; charity then increases our hope of heaven so that those who love God sing without ceasing: "Thy kingdom come, thy kingdom come!"

God loves those who love him. He bestows his graces

upon those who desire his love. Those who have the greatest love for God have absolute confidence in his goodness. This confidence creates the serene composure of the saints which helps them remain joyful and peaceful, even in the midst of the most severe trials. Their love for Jesus Christ and their faith in his generosity to those who love him help them to place all their confidence in him and so they find lasting peace. . . .

Saint Thomas defines Christian hope as a "sure expectation of eternal happiness." Its certainty stems from the infallible promise of God to give eternal life to his faithful servants. Charity, by removing sin, removes all obstacles to our possession of perfect happiness. The greater our love, therefore, the greater our hope of heaven. Those who love Jesus Christ intensely cannot help but desire and hope, as long as they remain on earth, to be united with their Lord in heaven. . . .

Love of my soul, I love you with my whole heart. I love you more than myself. I beg you to help me to love you ardently for the rest of my life. I long for the day when you will consume me with your love by showing me your infinite beauty. My dearest Redeemer, your merits are the essence of my hope.

The Life of Alphonsus Liguori

1696 - Born in Naples on Sep. 27

1713 - Earns law degree

1722 - Experiences conversion and makes private vow of celibacy; loses important court case

1723 - Begins studying for priesthood

1726 - Ordained; becomes popular preacher in Naples

1730 - Recommends new rule for sisters in convent in Scala

1731 - A sister in Scala envisions Alphonsus as leader of new order

1732 - Alphonsus leaves Naples to start new congregation

1747 - Congregation grows to 36 members in several houses

1748 - First, skeletal edition of *Moral Theology* appears in print

1749 - The Congregation of the Most Holy Redeemer receives papal approval

1750 - *The Glories of Mary* is published

1762 - Appointed Bishop of St. Agatha of the Goths

1775 - Resigns as bishop due to poor health

1779 - Unknowingly signs a vastly changed rule to obtain approval of the order from King of Naples

1780 - Pope Pius VI signs decree dismissing Alphonsus and members of the Congregation's house in Naples

1787 - Dies on Aug. 1

Painting by Leon Brune (1855) Photo by A. Fortier

Very Little Before God

Blessed Jeanne Jugan

1792 - 1879

Cancale, France, 1792: The great promise of the French Revolution of three years earlier had turned sour. Famine and unemployment increased, and roving bands of vagabonds searching for food caused great fear in the countryside. Disorder spread as the peasants turned on the aristocracy and burned the records of their debts and feudal obligations. By 1792, the church was suppressed and its property taken. Priests and religious were massacred. The king would be sent to the guillotine in January of 1793. No one felt safe.

Even remote Cancale, in the northwest province of Brittany, felt the revolution's aftershock. A sense of fear and oppression was everywhere, and the levels of crime and poverty rose dramatically. Then, there was the task of daily living. Most of the men were fishermen or merchant marines and thus, were often away for months at a time, trying to wrest a living from the sea. The sea could be merciless, however, creating many a widow and orphan. Consequently, the women of Cancale developed remarkable strength of character and determination of will.

On October 25, 1792, Jeanne Jugan was born in Cancale. Her father Joseph was a fisherman who—like so many others—spent much of his time plying his trade across the Atlantic in Newfoundland. Her mother, Marie, was a hardworking woman of tenacious faith, qualities she undoubtedly planned to instill in Jeanne once she was old enough.

But Jeanne was not to have the luxury of a long, pleasant childhood. In 1796, Joseph died at sea, and Marie went to work on a farm. As soon as she was able, Jeanne became a kitchen maid at a local manor home. Over time, she undertook the strenuous routine that characterized the lives of most young women of her time and place.

In 1816, when Jeanne was 23, something changed. She attended a mission in her parish, where many people recall her intensity of prayer and her deep attention to the homilies. Something inside Jeanne was coming to life; it was as if she were becoming a different person. Within a few months, Jeanne had the opportunity to test this "new person." A young man asked for her hand in marriage, and Jeanne declined. She had chosen to devote herself to the Lord, to serve Christ with her whole life. To her bewildered family, Jeanne explained, "God wants me for himself. He is keeping me for a work as yet unknown, for a work which is not yet founded."

A Calling Emerges

Moving to nearby Saint-Servan, Jeanne spent the next twenty-two years (1817-39) in various capacities: as a nurse, as a servant for well-to-do families, and as a companion to an elderly woman. She devoted all her time and attention to prayer, the sacraments, and a life of simplicity.

At the same time, she became increasingly concerned for the poor and the homeless. She would often go out of her way to help them—finding an extra blanket in the winter, providing a few potatoes during a hungry spell, or giving a word of comfort to the lonely. Because her life testified to her deep love for Christ and his people, many of the townsfolk came to respect this tall, slender woman from Cancale.

Around the close of 1839 (at the age of forty-seven), Jeanne informed her current employers that she would be leaving them: "I intend to devote myself to charitable work." A few days later, with the approval of the two women with whom she lived and prayed, Jeanne brought an aged blind woman, Anne Chauvin, into the apartment they shared. Jeanne gave Anne her bed, while she slept on the floor in the loft.

Not long afterward, she brought home Isabelle Coeuru, and Virginie Tredaniel, a younger roommate, gave up her bed. Jeanne's acts of generosity multiplied. She and Virginie and Marie Jamet, a friend of Virginie's, moved to a bigger flat, which they filled without delay. Soon afterward—thanks to the particular generosity of one friend—they bought an abandoned convent, where they could give the women better care and make room for the many more who would surely come.

A Life of Prayer and Service

Jeanne, Virginie, and Marie shared a growing love for Christ and a desire to consecrate themselves to him. Virginie and Marie saw themselves as Jeanne's disciples, learning from her a life of holiness and a commitment to serving Christ's people. Over time, Jeanne and her companions adopted a life of prayer and service.

The younger women took temporary vows of chastity and obedience to Jeanne. They all took a vow to live with their aged charges, not just to serve them out of a comfortable lifestyle. They first saw that the women were well fed, and only then did they eat the leftovers. Often, depending on the generosity of their patrons, only a few pieces of bread remained for them.

For the next twelve years, Jeanne threw herself into her work. Every day, she left home with a large basket over her arm and traveled the roads, begging door-to-door for her aged women. She began at Saint-Servan, but she soon saw a need in nearby Rennes. So she moved there and promptly founded a house.

From Rennes, she went to Dinan, then to Tours, and then to Angers. At each place, she followed the same pattern: Enter the town with nothing; in the name of Christ seek the aid of the townsfolk; rely on God's providence; and thank him for everything, good and bad. In each place, she established a foundation from nothing, a monumental task often accomplished in a matter of months.

Jeanne witnessed miracle after miracle. Much-needed funds or supplies often came in at the last minute. Food would arrive unannounced as the women gathered around an empty table, trusting in the Lord. Under Jeanne's care, elderly women known for their wasted lives came to embrace Christ and to part with sin. Even the hearts of many of the wealthy were softened: Jeanne's faith, humility, and determination often moved them to donate more than they intended—even more than she asked.

Development and Deprivation

Jeanne's two young companions shared a confessor, Fr. Auguste Le Pailleur. Impressed with their work, Fr. Le Pailleur foresaw the impact that this small group might have, and he offered his assistance. In May of 1842, the women, in the presence of Fr. Le Pailleur, established the Servants of the Poor and officially elected Jeanne superior. Marie, Virginie, and Madeleine Bourges—a recent addition—took a temporary vow of obedience to Jeanne.

The next year, the women renewed their vows and re-elected Jeanne as superior. Only two weeks later, however, Fr. Le Pailleur, using his clerical authority, invalidated the election. He replaced Jeanne with Marie Jamet—his own spiritual daughter. At the age of fifty-one, Jeanne became a common sister, submitted to Marie, her twenty-three-year-old protegée.

In time, Fr. Le Pailleur oversaw the almost complete rewriting of the congregation's history. He himself claimed to be the one who brought Anne Chauvin to Jeanne's home. He became the one who brought the women together, founding the congregation. Marie and Virginie became the first sisters, and Jeanne, the third woman to join. The only real recognition she received was of her success at collecting alms for houses that others supposedly founded.

Jeanne did not react harshly to Fr. Le Pailleur's actions. Through collecting, she had learned to accept everything as the providence and wisdom of God. Undaunted, she continued collecting for the aged poor in her homes. She was even called in to rescue the houses at Dinan and Tours from collapse. The people there needed reassurances that her sisters' work was just as authentic and pure as hers.

Once she won their confidence, Jeanne moved on. She may not have been head of the congregation affectionately referred to by most as the "Jeanne Jugans"—but her hard work and dedication kept it going in many places. And the work continually grew. Young women, touched by the witness of Jeanne's life, joined the congregation; and the aged poor found in Jeanne and her sisters the light and love of Christ, which had been missing from their lives for so long.

Sister Mary of the Cross

The year 1852 saw two important events. First, the congregation was officially recognized as a religious order within the church, with Fr. Le Pailleur named Father Superior-General. By this time, it was no small position: The order had 300 sisters working in fifteen houses, caring for over 1,500. Jeanne's dream—stolen from her in 1843—had surpassed her expectations.

The second important event immediately followed the first: Fr. Le Pailleur recalled Jeanne to the order's motherhouse and placed her in early retirement. She would now fade into the background, leaving him to take the foreground. Still very active at sixty years of age, Jeanne was given the small task of overseeing the novices' manual work. She would not even officially teach or counsel them. She would be known only by her religious name: Sister Mary of the Cross. Very few of the novices knew or even suspected that she was the legendary Jeanne Jugan.

Jeanne would now have twenty-seven years of obscurity and silence, "littleness," as she liked to call it. Yet it was during this period that many say she had the most profound influence on the order. Hundreds of young women came into contact with her during this time, and many point to the witness of her simplicity, her dependence on God's providence, and her deep love of Christ as the most memorable elements of their formation. Sister Mary of the Cross seemed to embody the ideals of the Little Sisters of the Poor.

When Jeanne died in obscurity on August 29, 1879, at the age of eighty-six, she was mourned only as Sister Mary of the Cross. By this time, the Little Sisters of the Poor numbered more than 2,400, with 170 houses throughout the world. A bit later, however, Fr. Le Pailleur's retelling of the congregation's history began to be uncovered, and in 1890, at the age of seventy-eight, he was removed from his position and called to the Vatican. He ended his days in the solitude of a small monastery. In 1893, as Marie Jamet was nearing death, she told a close friend, "I am not the first one, but I was told to act as though I were." Slowly the truth was righted, and Jeanne Jugan's name was restored.

During her hidden years, Jeanne often spent hours at a time kneeling in the chapel, gazing at the crucifix or the tabernacle of Christ's presence. Increasingly, her life testified to a peaceful and clear-minded surrender to Christ. Through her begging, Jeanne had learned to rely on God for everything.

The fact that the Little Sisters of the Poor relied only on their collecting, neither having a regular income nor owning any property other than the houses they inhabited, reflects Jeanne's early insistence that they live in faith and trust. Losing all earthly supports, all reliance on her talents and skills, Jeanne allowed God to work through her in a deeper, and even more powerful, way.

Grafted Onto the Cross

By enduring the trials of being silenced, having to give up her work, and having countless younger sisters not know who she was, Jeanne allowed the cross of Christ to put an end to the once headstrong, self-sufficient woman of Cancale. At one point, she told a well-informed novice, "Do not call me Jeanne Jugan. All that is left of her is Sister Mary of the Cross—unworthy though she is of that lovely name."

At another time, reflecting on her experiences, she was led to say, "We have been grafted onto the cross." Her life was not limited to the work she did; her worth did not depend on the success of her service. Rather, she learned with a greater clarity and depth the words of St. Paul: "Far be it from me to glory except in the cross of our Lord Jesus Christ" (Galatians 6:14).

We may be tempted to consider Jeanne's last twenty-seven years a waste of a valuable resource. On the other hand, we might compare her with Mary, the sister of Martha and Lazarus. When she poured out her precious perfume at the feet of Christ, "the house was filled with the fragrance of the ointment" (John 12:3). The disciples, upset at this action, said that the perfume's value would have been better spent on the poor (Mark 14:4-5), but Jesus corrected them: "She has done a beautiful thing to me. . . . Wherever the gospel is preached in the whole world, what she has done will be told in memory of her" (Mark 14:6,9).

In 1982, Pope John Paul II beatified Jeanne Jugan, another woman who "wasted herself" on Christ. Today, in nearly 220 homes in 30 countries, almost 3,600 Little Sisters of the Poor seek to follow Jeanne's example. They seek to pour out their lives before Jesus and to love his elderly poor in the same way that he loves them. By sacrificing their lives to the Lord and allowing him to prune them of every self-serving way, they strive to become "the aroma of Christ to God among those who are being saved" (2 Corinthians 2:15).

Very Little Before God

In 1844, the parish priest, the mayor, and fifteen municipal council members of Saint-Servan included this description of Jeanne and her work when they nominated her for a meritorious service award.

Who could do justice to this young woman's zeal in gathering in the poor! How often, herself going to seek them out in their dismal corners, she has persuaded them to go with her or, if they could not walk, has picked them up like a precious burden and cheerfully carried them off to her house! One day, she learns that an old man of seventy-two, Rodolphe Lainé, formerly a sailor, unpensioned, is living forsaken in a damp little cellar. She goes there, she sees a man with haggard face, covered in half-rotten rags, lying in what has once been straw but is now no more than a hideous dung-heap. This unfortunate had a stone for pillow; his cellar was underneath a house lived in by poor people who used to give him a few scraps of bread, and he had been living in this way for the previous two years. Moved by liveliest compassion at the sight, Jeanne went off, confided in a charitable acquaintance what she had just seen, and came back a moment later with a shirt and clean clothes. Having changed the old man's clothes, she takes this new guest back to her house, and today he enjoys good health. . . .

Stimulated by her example, three persons have joined her to share her cares and labors. These latter, with admirable devotedness and even to the detriment of their health, attend to all the heaviest jobs indoors, while outside Jeanne tirelessly subdivides herself into as many pieces as she has poor people to care for. She is forever on the go, whatever the weather, with a basket over her arm, and this she always brings home full. . . . In pleading their cause she is truly eloquent; she has often been known to burst into tears when explaining their needs. And so it is hard to refuse her, and she has nearly always succeeded in melting even the hardest of hearts. Even so, she is never importunate: if refused, she goes away at once, never showing the slightest sign of displeasure but saying, 'I'm sure you will help us another time.'

She has truly thrown in her lot with the poor; she dresses like them in what she is given; she lives on left-overs as they do, always making a point of keeping the best bits for those who are sick or more infirm; and the persons assisting her copy her example. . . .

Thus, by great effort and by the simple means which she has thought fit to adopt and which cause inconvenience to no one, Jeanne Jugan has not only won the confidence of the town but has succeeded in snatching sixty-five old people from cold and want, has rid our streets of the hideous spectacle of their beggary and in less than four years has laid the foundations of a proper hospice or, as it is generally called, a home for the aged and infirm poor.

We have thought it our duty to describe to the Members responsible for allocating the awards for merit, some part of the good which this poor woman is doing, and if their favourable judgment sees fit to recognize such zeal and charity, we for our part are sure that the reward bestowed on her will contribute further to the welfare of her beloved poor.

The Life of Jeanne Jugan

1792 - Born on Oct. 25 in Cancale, France

1796 - Her father dies

1808–1816 - Works as kitchen maid at local manor house

1816 - Attends parish mission and chooses celibate life

1817–1839 - Leaves Cancale to live in Saint-Servan; works as nurse, servant, and companion to an older woman

1839 - Leaves her job and takes two elderly women into her home

1841 - With two friends, moves into larger quarters and takes in more elderly

1842 - Establishes Servants of the Poor with her companions and is chosen as superior

1843 - Re-elected superior, but Fr. Le Pailleur overrules her and designates a younger sister as superior

1844 - Name of congregation is changed to Little Sisters of the Poor

1846 - Houses in Rennes and Dinan open

1852 - Congregation is officially recognized as a religious order and grows to 300 sisters in 15 houses; Jeanne is summoned to order's motherhouse and placed in early retirement

1879 - Dies on Aug. 29

God's Clear Light of Love

Saint Clare of Assisi

1193 - 1253

To her many friends and admirers, Clare of Assisi was a model of medieval womanhood. Born around 1193 into one of Assisi's noble families, she seemed to flourish naturally in an environment of privilege and prestige. Her father, Favarone, was an accomplished warrior-knight, and her mother, Ortulana, was known both for her ability to manage her extensive household and for her personal piety and charity. Consequently, Clare possessed her mother's refined spirit and her father's courageous determination. She was also one of the most beautiful young women of Assisi. Many were the young knights and merchants' sons who sought her favor, vying for her hand in marriage.

From her earliest years, however, something different was stirring in Clare. Unlike the storybook princesses we are all familiar with, her life was not one of minor adventures followed by a great "happily ever after." She lived through a terrible war between Assisi and Perugia, was sent into temporary exile with her mother and sisters, and lost her father in battle while she was still young. All of these experiences combined to produce in her a strength of character and a reliance on God that would last her whole life.

As Clare approached marrying age, her uncle Monaldo began to consider who might be an appropriate husband for her. He wanted someone who could not only care for her, but whose wealth would bring greater security and honor to the family name. Clare resisted. Growing within her was a desire to be united with no man, so that she could be united more fully with Jesus, whose love far surpassed any other love she could know. Eventually, much to Monaldo's chagrin, Clare took a private vow of virginity and sold her family inheritance, giving the money to Assisi's poor. There could be no turning back: She still had her physical beauty, but she had relinquished her wealth and social standing.

Clare had embraced a life of simplicity, but she wanted to go further in committing herself to the Lord. She had heard about Francis, the young would-be knight who had also left his family's wealth to live in poverty. He spent his time begging food for the poor, repairing churches, and preaching in Assisi's public plazas. Francis too had heard about Clare's courageous acts of charity and her love for the Lord. Eventually, the two met and a brother-sister relationship quickly developed. Clare went often to Francis, to hear him preach, to seek his advice, and to pray with him. Over time, her desire to adopt Francis' way grew, until she made the final break with her old life.

On the night of Palm Sunday, 1212, Clare stole out of her uncle's house and met Francis and his friars at one of his churches. There, following ancient tradition, Francis cut Clare's lovely hair and clothed her in a coarse habit. With those acts, Clare embraced a new life. Leaving her home in the world, she found a home with Christ as she began a life of austerity and prayer in the convent of San Damiano, the same place where Francis heard Jesus tell him to rebuild the church.

As news of Clare's decision spread, other women joined her, and a community of prayer and service formed around her. The "Poor Ladies," as they became known, lived in utter simplicity, owning absolutely nothing, so that they could rely on God to provide for them as he had promised he would. This was the first time in church history that an order of women lived in such radical poverty, and it met with much opposition. Not only family members, but even bishops and popes warned Clare that she was being too idealistic, that the gospel's demands shouldn't be taken so literally. How could she care for her sisters when they had absolutely no security or protection? Yet, despite these questions, Clare remained serene and determined.

Clare chose such a radical path for one reason: This embrace of poverty best enabled her to imitate Christ. He was her goal, not the lifestyle, and it was his simplicity of heart, his poverty of spirit, and his intimate love for the Father, that motivated her. In a letter to Agnes, a Bohemian princess who had chosen to follow her example, Clare wrote:

> If so great and good a Lord, then, on coming into the Virgin's womb, chose to appear despised, needy, and

> poor in this world, so that people who were in . . . absolute need of heavenly nourishment might become rich in him by possessing the kingdom of heaven, then rejoice and be glad! Be filled with a remarkable happiness and a spiritual joy! (*First Letter to Agnes of Prague*, 19-20)

As she read the gospels, Clare saw in Jesus the freedom and spontaneity of spirit that flowed from his poverty. Because he had separated himself from the complexities of the world, Jesus could relate more intimately with his Father. He could know his Father's will, receive his love, and bring his life to others. Living with the comfort and protection of the Father, he could spread that love to others, through miracles and healings, and in the parables and discourses he preached.

As a result of her imitation of Christ, Clare began to reflect his attributes in greater measure—at times with astonishing results. The story is told that in September of 1240, during a Saracen invasion of Assisi, some soldiers had begun to climb the walls of her convent, looking for the women. On hearing of the threat, Clare threw herself before the Blessed Sacrament and cried out, "Does it please you, my Lord, to deliver into the hands of the pagans your defenseless handmaids whom I have nourished with your love? O Lord, I beg you to defend these your servants whom I am in this hour unable to defend!" Then, Clare and those with her heard a small voice reply, "I will always defend you." With that, she told her sisters not to panic, and within moments the soldiers "quickly clambered over the walls they had scaled, being routed by the power of her prayers" (*Legend of St. Clare*, 22).

Clare died in 1253, just two days after she obtained from Pope Innocent IV the "Privilege of Poverty." For almost forty years, she had fought with humble determination to secure the promise that her Poor Ladies would be free to live in radical poverty and simplicity, never seeking nor being forced to accept the protection of an institution, however holy or well-endowed. Like Mother Teresa's sisters today and like Francis in her own time, Clare wanted to be a mirror of Christ, reflecting his heart of humility, love, and service. Her reflection not only changed thirteenth-century Europe, but continues to draw others today into the clear light of Christ.

God's Clear Light of Love

This excerpt is taken from Clare's third letter to Agnes of Prague, the daughter of the King of Bohemia.

I can rejoice truly—and no one can rob me of such joy—because I now possess what under heaven I have desired. For I see that, helped by a special gift of wisdom from the mouth of God himself and in an awe-inspiring and unexpected way, you have brought to ruin the subtleties of our crafty enemy and the pride that destroys human nature and the vanity that infatuates human hearts.

I see, too, that by humility, the virtue of faith, and the strong arms of poverty, you have taken hold of that *incomparable treasure hidden in the field* of the world and in the hearts of men (Matthew 13:44), with which you have purchased that field of him by whom all things have been made from nothing. And, to use the words of the Apostle himself in their proper sense, I consider you a *co-worker of God* himself (see 1 Corinthians 3:9; Romans 16:3) and a support of the weak members of his ineffable body. Who is there, then, who would not encourage me to rejoice over such marvelous joys?

Therefore, dearly beloved, may you too *always rejoice in the Lord* (Philippians 4:4). And may neither bitterness nor a cloud of sadness overwhelm you, O dearly beloved Lady in Christ, joy of the angels, and crown of your sisters!

Place your mind before the mirror of eternity!
Place your soul in *the brilliance of glory!*
Place your heart in *the figure of the* divine *substance!*
And transform your whole being into the image of the
Godhead itself through contemplation!

So that you too may feel what his friends feel
as they taste *the hidden sweetness*
which God himself has reserved
from the beginning
for those who love him.

Since you have cast aside all those things which, in this deceitful and turbulent world, ensnare their blind lovers, love him totally who gave himself totally for your love. His beauty the sun and moon admire, and of his gifts there is no limit in abundance, preciousness, and magnitude. I am speaking of him who is the Son of the Most High, whom the Virgin brought to birth and remained a virgin after his birth. Cling to his most sweet Mother who carried a Son whom the heavens could not contain; and yet she carried him in the little enclosure of her holy womb and held him on her virginal lap. . . .

Therefore, as the glorious Virgin of virgins carried [Christ] materially in her body, you too, *by following in his footprints* (see 1 Peter 2:21), especially those of poverty and humility, can, without any doubt, always carry him spiritually in your chaste and virginal body. And you will hold him by whom you and *all things are held together* (see Wisdom 1:7; Colossions 1:17), thus possessing that which, in comparison with the other transitory possessions of this world, you will possess more securely. How many kings and queens of this world let themselves be deceived! For, even though their pride may reach the skies and their heads through the clouds, in the end they are as forgotten as a dung-heap!

The Life of Clare of Assisi

c. 1193 - Born in Assisi into a noble family

1199 - During a war, goes into exile with her mother and sisters

1209 - Francis' rule receives verbal approval from Pope Innocent III

1210 - Gives her inheritance to the poor and makes a private vow of virginity

1212 - Leaves her uncle's house on Palm Sunday night and begins a new life in monastery of San Damiano

1215 - Francis gives the "Poor Ladies" a "Form of Life"; Clare accepts role as abbess of San Damiano

1216 - Pope Innocent III grants the Poor Ladies of San Damiano the "Privilege of Property," the right to live as a community without property

1219 - Cardinal Hugolino issues a rule based on St. Benedict, but not including the Privilege of Poverty that Clare desires

1226 - Francis dies

1234 - Writes first letter to Agnes of Prague

1240 - Saracens invade the Monastery of San Damiano, but leave without harming anyone after Clare prays

1247 - Pope Innocent IV renews Rule of 1219

1253 - On Aug. 9, Pope Innocent IV approves a rule written by Clare that restores the "Privilege of Poverty." Clare dies on Aug. 11 at San Damiano

A Dream Come True

Saint John Bosco

1815 - 1888

In 1824, in a small village in northern Italy, a nine-year-old boy dreamt that he was standing in a field, surrounded by a crowd of other young boys who were playing and shouting, pouring their energy into their activity. Not far away, he saw another group of boys fighting each other, yelling and cursing the whole time.

Because he was a naturally energetic and somewhat reckless boy, he charged into this group, yelling for them to stop. They ignored him, and so in frustration, he tried to beat all of them into submission. Naturally, all the boys turned and laid into him with their fists.

Suddenly, a tall, noble-looking man dressed in shining white came toward them. Everyone stopped. "You'll never help these boys by beating them," he told the lad. "Be kind and gentle. Lead them and teach them how evil sin is and how desirable virtue is. Then they will become your friends."

Confused, the boy asked, "Who are you? Why are you telling me such impossible things?" But the man gave a cryptic answer and disappeared. The boys around him immediately changed into a pack of wolves. They were growling and snapping at each other when a woman appeared, dressed in a golden, glittering cloak. She took the boy's hand and told him not to fear, "What I am about to do for these animals you will do for all of my children." Immediately the wolves turned into lambs, bleating and jumping playfully around the woman. "You will only succeed at this if you learn to become humble and strong," she told him.

Bewildered and frightened, the boy burst into tears. "I don't understand!" he cried. "Don't worry," she replied. "You will understand it all in good time." With that, the boy awoke. He was bathed in sweat, and his fists were sore from being clenched so tightly.

Determination

This was the first of countless visions and prophetic dreams of John Bosco, an uneducated farmboy. During the next sixty-four years, this dream would recur occasionally, reminding him and impelling him along the path that God had marked out. Every other dream and vision flowed from this one promise of rough boys transformed into lambs through his work.

Soon after his dream, John decided that he was indeed called to work with boys, to lead them to Christ, and to care for them. He had received a vision, a goal for his life, and with characteristic determination, he committed himself to taking all the necessary steps to bring about its fulfillment. And for John, the dream was immense. Eventually it would extend far beyond a youth group in a parish to encompass millions of young people who would be transformed by the Spirit and dedicated to the gospel. His calling was great, and John sought to answer the calling with faith and trust, embracing it with all his energy.

For the next seventeen years, Bosco threw himself into studies, preparing for the priesthood and the fulfillment of his calling. At every step along his path, he encountered difficulties: lack of money; strong, often violent, opposition from his stepbrother; teachers who scorned him because of his age; and poverty.

Keeping God's vision alive, John saw in each step an opportunity to practice the lesson of his dream—that it would not be by violent, aggressive action, but by faith and trust in God that he would see his dream fulfilled. So John persevered, fixing his eyes on God's plan and his heart on the words spoken to him.

"A Friend of Mine"

After his ordination in June of 1841, Bosco moved to Turin, where he undertook a program of advanced seminary studies. Almost immediately, his calling began to set down permanent roots. Only five weeks after he began classes, as he was preparing to say Mass one day, he heard a commotion in the sacristy. He investigated and saw the old sacristan, Comotti, wielding a rod over a young ruffian.

As Comotti began raining down blows on the boy, Bosco ran to interrupt. "What's going on?" he demanded. Seizing the opportunity, the boy fled. Comotti replied hotly, "I found him in my sacristy, and when I told him to serve Mass, he said he didn't know how. I won't have street urchins cluttering up my church!" "Bring him back," Bosco said. "He's a friend of mine." Comotti replied, "That wretch?" "Yes," said John. "Any boy in trouble is my friend."

Chagrined, Comotti retrieved the boy.

"What's your name, son?" Bosco asked.

"Bart Garelli."

"Where are you from, Bart?"

"Asti."

"What's your job?"

"Bricklayer."

"Are your parents alive?"

"No, both dead."

"How old are you?"

"Sixteen."

"Can you read or write?"

"No."

"Can you sing or whistle?"

The boy broke into a smile.

"Sure!"

"Tell me, Bart, have you made your first Communion?"

"No, not yet."

"Have you ever been to Confession?"

"Only a long time ago, when I was a little boy."

"Do you pray?"

"I don't know how to pray."

"Do you go to catechism classes?"

"No, I'm ashamed to. All the other kids are younger than

me and they know a lot more than I do."

"Well, what if I taught you catechism? Would you come?"

"I'd be very glad to."

"When do you want to begin?"

"Whenever you say."

"How about tonight?"

"Okay."

"How about right now, after Mass?"

"If you like."

After Mass, Don Bosco ("Don" is an Italian title of respect often given to priests) gave Bart his first lesson. He told him to come back the next week, which he did, this time accompanied by eight other friends, all similarly tough teenagers. Bosco gladly accepted them, and from this small beginning, a group rapidly grew. Within a year, he was teaching more than a hundred boys about Jesus and how to pray.

Bosco had always been an energetic, fun-loving man himself, and so, when he wanted to offer the boys a safe, constructive outlet for their energy, he took it upon himself to organize and participate in numerous games, sporting events, and competitions. Few of the boys had ever dreamed that a priest could be so lively and approachable.

From Dream to Reality

Most of Bosco's boys were either orphans or had left their homes in the mountains to find work in the city. Almost every one was poor; many were homeless and unemployed. Most of them lived in horrible conditions—crammed into basements, or out on the streets, sleeping in alleys and abandoned yards. The more Bosco learned of these wretched conditions, the more his heart went out to the boys, and the harder he worked to reach as many as possible.

He once told a friend, "Familiarity breeds affection and affection breeds confidence. It opens the heart, and young people approach their teachers, assistants, and superiors without fear." His own life testifies to the truth of this statement. Virtually all of the boys who came to him grew to love and respect this stocky, tousled-haired priest who was never without a smile and a kind word for them, even if he was admonishing them.

Over the years, even though they were viewed by many with suspicion and hostility, their numbers grew. By 1847, he was working with more than 600 boys. Every Sunday they would gather for prayer, confession, Mass, and games. During the week, he met many in smaller groups, teaching them about Jesus, giving them reading and writing lessons, or helping them learn a trade by which they could earn a living.

Bosco wanted his "Festive Oratory" (as he called his work with the boys) to become an instrument of conversion and formation, a comprehensive educational institution, praised by the secular government and blessed by the Church. And so it became. Angry, lonely, violent castaways who came to him, were converted to Christ through this spiritual man's witness of humility, strength, and faith. Many became teachers, priests, and public servants.

They all loved Bosco and willingly opened their hearts to him, confessing their sins, and asking his advice. He made it a point to hear each boy's confession at least once a month, helping them experience the peace and freedom of repentance as well as the assurance that comes from opening their hearts to God and to an elder whom they could trust. Quite a few were moved to join the religious order he founded, the Society of Saint Francis de Sales (the Salesians), rather than a more established and respected order like the Franciscans or Dominicans.

For years, Don Bosco was aware that a similar type of work was needed for poor girls who were homeless or on their own. Always convinced that he was intended to work directly only with boys, Bosco waited patiently until he was sure that this undertaking was God's will. Finally, on August 5, 1872, the Daughters of Mary, Help of Christians, was formed, and Mary Mazzarello, a longtime friend of Bosco's, was named its superior.

These women cared for young girls just as Bosco's men took care of the boys—in evangelization, education, and training. Bosco sent his first group of missionaries to South America in 1875, and two years later, some of these sisters joined them. Together they pushed into the southern, primitive region of Patagonia. The Daughters of Mary were the first group of women religious to work in the jungle.

A Burden and a Joy

In the midst of all his work with the boys, Don Bosco saw to the writing and publication of more than 150 books, novels, and pamphlets on education, youth, and the Christian life. He built magnificent churches in Turin and Rome, ran a religious order, and oversaw missionary work around the world. He was a much sought-after counselor, both by popes and heads of state. Constantly in debt, he always trusted in God's provision. By his own choice, out of love for God, he willingly worked himself to near exhaustion in order to keep up with the responsibilities that the Lord had given him.

Don Bosco never complained about his difficulties or sought to lighten his load; he always wore a smile. He recognized that these pressures were God's way of teaching him the difference between trying to do godly work with human effort and learning to trust in God. God is always looking for humble, teachable servants, and Bosco was determined to be one. He was constantly making plans to bring about the fulfillment of the visions he had received.

Quite often, his friends and coworkers would accuse him of dreaming too much and wanting to accomplish too many things with too few resources. But in each case, his reply was, "If it is God's will, how can it fail? If it is not God's calling, he will make it clear to me. I don't need to worry about anything else."

The Preventive System

For Don Bosco, teaching and caring for young people was not a matter of punishment and harsh discipline. His first objective was to win their confidence and trust. Through sports, a card game, or in the Sacrament of Confession, he sought to become "all things" to them (1 Corinthians 9:22), wanting each boy to experience the love of God and new life in Christ personally.

Bosco taught them catechism—the doctrines of Christianity—but for most of them, the real change came when they saw how he lived out these doctrines. His demeanor consistently reflected a deep love for Christ, an experience of God that they all hungered for. In a letter commenting on what is needed to win young people to the Lord, he wrote:

> How often in my long life I have had to learn and relearn [this] great truth! It is much easier to get angry than to be patient, to threaten a child than to persuade him. Our impatient pride prefers to punish the headstrong rather than to correct them with firm and tender patience.

It was not just a dream that enabled John Bosco to change wild animals into tame lambs. In his dream, he began by flailing about with his fists, thus providing an insight into the lessons he had to learn. He could not act in anger or rashness; he had to learn to refuse the temptations of pride and self-importance that accompanied success. He sought to let the Lord teach him how to love young people with the same love that Jesus had for them. He asked God to reveal his sin to him, and, through repentance and faith, he allowed the Lord to make him a willing, humble instrument of his work.

This was the heart of what Bosco called "the preventive system" of education: Keep young people productively occupied. Leave them no opportunity to dream idly or to experiment with temptation. Help them see the destructive nature of the "little sins" they commit early on, so that the bigger, more devastating possibilities are more surely avoided. Encourage them to help each other and to work together. Through creative games and hard work, teach them to rely on one another. Above all, by your concern for them and your own relationship with Christ, give them an attractive testimony of the life you want them to embrace. In following these steps, Bosco knew he was precluding many deeper problems and sins from corrupting their lives.

John Bosco died on January 31, 1888, at the age of seventy-two. He left behind him a legacy of thousands of boys converted to Christ, many of whom became zealous preachers and missionaries. His educational philosophy was hailed as both innovative and successful. Through the Salesians and the Daughters of Mary, Help of Christians, his love for the gospel spread throughout the world. The dream of his youth became a reality. In peace, he closed his eyes and entered the most real and glorious dream he had ever known. Don Bosco, father to so many, was welcomed as a beloved son into the inheritance of Christ.

A Dream Come True

John Bosco's dreams often revealed his future work.
He spoke about this dream in 1864,
after his Salesian order had been established.

One day, in 1847, I had been meditating for some time on the best way to do good, especially to young people, when the Queen of Heaven appeared to me and led me into an enchanting garden. It had a rustic, but immense and beautiful porch. Climbing vines adorned it, coiled and reached upward, interlacing like a curtain. Rosebushes in full bloom grew on either side. The ground, too, was covered with roses.

"Take off your shoes!" she said. When I had done so, she added, "Walk down that rose arbor. That is the road you have to travel."

I was glad I had removed my shoes, for the roses were so beautiful, I would have been sorry to trample them. I started walking, but immediately felt that the roses had very sharp thorns to them. My feet began to bleed. After walking a few steps, I had to go back.

"I need my shoes," I told my guide.

"You'll need good shoes," she agreed.

I put on my shoes again and returned to the road, this time together with a number of companions who suddenly appeared to ask if they could go with me. They followed me under the beautiful arbor which now became narrower and lower. Many of the branches reached to the ground and then rose up again like streamers; still others hung over the path, but all were covered with roses, and I saw only roses around, above and below me. I still felt sharp pains in my feet and began to limp. . . . Nevertheless, I went forward while my legs got scratched and became entangled in the branches on the ground. Each time I pushed aside a branch, or leaned against the trellis to avoid it, the thorns pricked me so that not only my hands but my whole body started to bleed. The hanging roses also concealed thorns which pierced my head.

"Don Bosco always walks on roses!" said those who were watching. I called on seminarians, priests and lay people to follow me and these, drawn by the beauty of the flowers, did so with pleasure. But they quickly discovered that they had to walk over sharp thorns hidden everywhere. "We've been deceived!" they cried. . . . I was encouraged, however, when another group of seminarians, priests and laymen came toward me. "We are all yours," they said, "and ready to follow you.". . .

Our Lady, who had been my guide, asked me: "Do you know the meaning of what you now see?" . . .

"No," I said. "Please explain it to me."

"The road you followed among the roses and thorns represents the care you are to take of young people. To travel along it you must wear the shoes of mortification. The thorns underfoot represent the human likes and dislikes which distract an educator from his purpose, which wound him, keep him from fulfilling his mission and from earning for himself an eternal reward. The roses are symbols of the love which should distinguish you and your fellow-workers; the thorns represent the various obstacles, sufferings and disappointments you will encounter. But never lose heart. With self-denial and with love you will overcome every difficulty and finally reach the roses without thorns."

The Life of John Bosco

1815 - Born in Murialdo in northern Italy

1817 - His father dies

1824 - Has a dream about subduing unruly boys, indicating his future vocation

1835 - Enters the seminary

1841 - Ordained on Jun. 5

1841-1844 - Moves to Turin for advanced studies; begins work with youth

1846 - Finds a permanent place for boys in Valdocco, which he transforms into an Oratory

1847 - Opens a second Oratory

1862 - Twenty-two candidates make public vows for Bosco's new religious society, to be known as the Salesians

1863 - Opens first school outside Turin, marking a period of rapid growth and expansion of the order

1866 - Work is completed on the Salesian church in Valdocco, the Church of Mary, Help of Christians

1872 - A congregation to care for young girls, the Daughters of Mary, Help of Christians, is formed

1875 - The first Salesian missionaries set off for South America

1888 - Dies on Jan. 31

Caring for the Forgotten

Blessed Katharine Drexel

1858 - 1955

Katharine Drexel grew up in the luxury of nineteenth-century high society, the daughter of wealthy but devout parents. Along with her parents and sisters, Katharine resided in a stately home in Center City Philadelphia, "summered" at delightful country estates outside the city, made extensive tours of both the United States and Europe, and studied at home with the best private tutors.

At the age of 30, however, this prayerful and business-savvy woman decided to channel her considerable wealth and talent into service for those who had been marginalized by American society—Native and African Americans. Long before the Civil Rights movement was born, "Mother Drexel" dedicated herself to overcoming the evils of racial discrimination and poverty. Her compassion for the suffering and her love for Christ had enabled her to detect those injustices before the rest of the nation awakened to them.

Beyond social justice, Mother Katharine wanted souls for Christ, whom she loved so deeply. Her interior life, centered on devotion to the Blessed Sacrament, was the fuel that enabled her to work unceasingly for her less fortunate brothers and sisters. During the last two decades of her life, after she had retired, her intense desire for a quiet contemplative life was finally realized.

A Spirit of Generosity

Katharine Mary Drexel was born on November 26, 1858; four weeks later her mother died. Katharine's older sister Elizabeth was just three years old at the time. Katharine's father, Francis A. Drexel—who presided over an international banking empire that his father had launched—remarried two years later. Emma Bouvier Drexel, the daughter of a prestigious Catholic family in Philadelphia, embraced the two girls as her own and soon gave birth to a third daughter, Louise. Tragedy struck again in 1879, when Emma—who had taught the girls to be generous—was diagnosed with cancer. For three years, Katharine nursed her stepmother through intense physical pain, and it was during this time that the idea of a religious vocation first visited her.

Emma's death in early 1883 revealed to Katharine the transitory nature of earthly life in a dramatic way. On a European tour in 1884, as she gazed at the beauty of the great cities, she wrote to her spiritual director, Bishop James O'Connor:

> Like the little girl who wept when she found that her doll was stuffed with sawdust and her drum was hollow, I, too,

> have made a horrifying discovery. . . . I have ripped both the doll and the drum open and the fact lies plainly and in all its glaring reality before me: All, all, all (there is no exception) is passing away and will pass away.

This sentiment intensified when Katharine's father died unexpectedly in 1885. Ten percent of his vast fortune was given to his favorite Catholic charities; the remaining $14 million—a staggering amount of money a century ago—was put in a trust, the annual income to be divided among the three daughters. Now Katharine was in a position to begin her own charitable works. Two missionaries approached her about the need for financial assistance to Catholic missions to the Indians. Katharine had always been interested in bringing Christ to the Native Americans, and she was moved by the dire poverty that the missionaries described. She began giving large amounts to support the building of Catholic missions and schools for them and made several visits out West to ensure that the money was being spent wisely.

"A Void in My Heart"

In the meantime, Katharine continued to wrestle with her desire for a religious vocation. Bishop O'Connor was dead set against such a decision. "You are doing more for the Indians now, than any religious, or even any religious community has ever done, or perhaps, ever could do for them in this country." He advised her to "think, pray, wait."

Katharine found the bishop's direction increasingly difficult to follow. "As far as I can read my heart, I am not happy in the world," she replied. "There is a void in my heart that only God can fill. Can God obtain full possession of my heart while I live in the world?" She longed for the contemplative life, leaving others to dispense her wealth while she prayed, did penance, and above all, received the Eucharist daily.

The three Drexel sisters went on another tour of Europe in 1887, during which Pope Leo XIII granted them a private audience. Katharine was trying to find an order of priests to staff the Indian missions, and she summoned the courage to plead with the Pope. He responded, "Why not, my child, yourself become a missionary?"

Finally, Katharine could no longer contain the deepest desire of her heart. In November 1888, she wrote Bishop O'Connor to say that she could refuse the Lord no longer. "It appears to me, Reverend Father, that I am not obliged to submit my judgment to yours, as I have been doing for two years, for I feel so sad in doing it . . . so restless because my heart is not rested in God." The bishop capitulated. Katharine had held up "under the long and severe tests" to which he had subjected her, and he withdrew his opposition.

A New Congregation

A few months later, Bishop O'Connor suggested that Katharine establish a new order for "the Indian and Colored people." Katharine was overwhelmed. "The responsibility of such a call almost crushes me, because I am so infinitely poor in the virtues necessary," she wrote. After praying for another month, however, she acceded to the bishop's suggestion. In May 1889, Katharine entered the Sisters of Mercy in Pittsburgh for formation. Her doubts accompanied her, but Bishop O'Connor assured her, "I am not surprised to find you dreading and shrinking somewhat from the responsibility of the undertaking. If you did not, I should feel very nervous about your success."

Before her final profession as the first member of the Sisters of the Blessed Sacrament, Katharine lost the man who had been her constant support. In May of 1890, after a long illness, Bishop O'Connor died. A close friend of Bishop O'Connor's, Archbishop P. J. Ryan of Philadelphia, stepped in to fill the void. Katharine selected a site nineteen miles outside of Philadelphia to build the motherhouse for the community, even as she mourned the unexpected death of her sister Elizabeth, who had only recently married.

While the motherhouse was under construction, Mother Katharine and her thirteen new members moved to the Drexel summer home and began their training. The rule being drafted for the new community permitted daily Communion, something uncommon at that time, but a grace Katharine had deeply desired. In 1894, after extensive formation in prayer, humility, and service, nine sisters were sent to staff a school Katharine had funded as a laywoman: St. Catherine's in Santa Fe, New Mexico.

The Active Apostolate

Thus began the work that Mother Katharine would oversee for the next forty years. She crisscrossed the country numerous times—often under grueling conditions—to direct the building of missions and schools and to encourage her sisters to draw ever closer to Jesus. In her mind, Catholic education served a twofold purpose: It equipped minority children with the necessary skills to lift themselves out of poverty, and it formed their faith, bringing them Christ through the Eucharist.

From the missions in the West, Mother Katharine went south to help educate black children who were barred from attending school with white children. In Nashville, she had to use a third party to purchase an estate in a white part of town to avoid community opposition to a school for black girls. When the plans for the school were revealed, an uproar ensued. There was even an attempt to build a street through the estate to render it useless! Quietly but determinedly, Katharine continued her work, and the school opened without incident.

From the South, the congregation eventually moved north to establish schools in the urban ghettos of cities such as New York and Chicago. The 18,000 letters stored at the motherhouse are a testament to the business negotiations, projects, and plans that Mother Katharine undertook during those years. Busy as she was, however, Mother Katharine did not neglect the contemplative life she valued so highly. When her sisters had left the motherhouse chapel, she often remained behind with arms extended in the form of a cross, her eyes fixed on the crucifix, tears streaming down her face.

The demanding pace Mother Katharine set for herself ended in 1935, when at the age of seventy-seven, she suffered a severe heart attack. She spent the last twenty years of her life in quiet prayer and intercession. The privilege of Mass in her room was granted, and the altar at which she had received her First Communion was installed there. She died peacefully on March 3, 1955, leaving a congregation with ministries all over the country serving Native and African Americans. One of the last meditations she wrote expressed the driving force behind all her work:

> Practical conclusion: Love! Love! Let us give ourselves to real pure love. Devotion to the Sacred Heart is a devotion which alone can banish the coldness of our time. The renewal which I seek and which we all seek is a work of love and can be accomplished by love alone.

Pope John Paul II beatified Mother Katharine Drexel in 1988, and her cause for canonization continues. Katharine took the words of Jesus literally to "sell what you possess give to the poor . . . and follow me" (Matthew 19:21). Faithful to her vow of poverty, Katharine wrote letters on scrap paper and drank day-old coffee to save money. At her death in 1955, Mother Katharine had used the money she inherited to establish 145 Catholic missions and 12 schools for Native Americans, and 50 schools for blacks, most of which were staffed by the congregation she founded—the Sisters of the Blessed Sacrament.

Caring for the Forgotten

From a letter by Katharine Drexel written after visiting her sisters at St. Michael's School on a Navajo reservation in Arizona.

I wish I had some more days to spend with you, I much feared I failed to express the real consolation my visit was to me. Do you know it seemed like the realization of years, yes, longings of the last fifteen years? When I looked at you, the virgin mothers of the poor Navajos, my heart was full of gratitude to God because he had, beyond all expectation, fulfilled the desires he himself had given me, to do something for these poor pagans. You know God gave me this desire one or two years before I entered religion or ever dreamed that God would permit me to be a sister.

And so, on this visit I looked up in wonder at God's wonderful ways and thought how little we imagine what may be the result of listening and acting on a desire he puts into the heart. If he puts it into the heart, he will bless it, if we try to act upon it, and great will be the effect before God. It will be success before God, even if it be not so to our weak understanding. For God means that which he breathes into the soul should bring forth fruit to eternal life. God in his great condescension to my weakness has let me see with my own eyes the good results of this desire of fifteen years ago. When one is strong in the spiritual life he does not always permit this. He makes us adore without understanding.

How fifteen years ago, could I have believed that eleven of my own spiritual daughters would be amongst the Navajos and that each one of them would have a mother's heart for them. That, God has given to you, along with big earnest desires for the salvation of your spiritual children, the Navajos. These are the desires God has placed in your hearts and great will be the effort if you continue as you do, to nourish these desires and act upon them. He will fulfill your desires with good things far beyond your expectations, especially as you have so cheerfully endured the sacrifices of the foundation of this Convent. . . . With God's help you were able to get through last winter's privations. Years ago you would not have believed you would have had the strength. Who gave you the strength? God! He will give you more strength this year.

The Life of Katharine Drexel

1858 - Born on Nov. 26 in Philadelphia; her mother dies a month later

1860 - Her father, Frank, marries Emma Bouvier

1883 - Emma dies after a long illness; Katharine first considers religious life

1885 - Her father dies; she begins contributing to the Indian missions

1887 - Meets Pope Leo XIII, who suggests she become a missionary

1888 - Decides to become a nun. Bishop James O'Connor, her spiritual director, encourages her to establish a new order of sisters

1889 - Enters the Sisters of Mercy in Pittsburgh for formation

1890 - Her close friend and spiritual director, O'Connor, dies

1891 - Becomes the first professed member of her new congregation, Sisters of the Blessed Sacrament

1894 - Nine sisters are sent to staff their first school in New Mexico

1907 - Vatican gives conditional approval to the rule of the Sisters of the Blessed Sacrament

1935 - Suffers a severe heart attack and retires from active leadership of the community

1955 - Dies at the motherhouse in Cornwells Heights, Pennsylvania, on Mar. 3

Scala/Art Resource, NY

Champion of the Incarnation

Saint Athanasius

298 - 373

Just after midnight, in February of the year 356, the Bishop of Alexandria in Egypt was conducting a crowded vigil service. Suddenly the church was surrounded by armed soldiers of the Emperor Constantius. The bishop calmed his people and asked a deacon to read Psalm 136. After every verse, the believers all responded, "His mercy endures forever." Finally, the soldiers burst into the church and attempted to seize the bishop. His clergy urged him to escape, but he refused until he saw that most of the congregation had safely left the church. Then, under what he believed was divine protection, the bishop was able to slip out unnoticed and escape into hiding.

Thus began the third exile for Athanasius—one which was to last six years. Two more exiles would follow. By the end of his life, Athanasius had spent sixteen of his forty-five years as a bishop in exile. A man of strong will and irrepressible humor, Athanasius devoted himself to preserving the truth of the gospel. This was particularly challenging for Athanasius because the church in his time had just been recognized and embraced by the Roman emperors. As a result, it was faced with a new type of power struggle and identity crisis.

Athanasius was born in approximately 298 in Alexandria, Egypt, to a Christian family. As a child, he received a classical Greek education and solid theological formation; he also witnessed one of the last and most severe persecutions of Christians under the pagan emperor Diocletian. This experience of seeing his friends martyred—and facing the possibility of martyrdom himself—left a deep impression on him. The fact that so many men and women were willing to give up their lives for Christ only strengthened this young man's trust that Jesus had truly destroyed death.

The Mystery of the Incarnation

Around the time that he was ordained a deacon, in 318, Athanasius wrote a theological treatise, *On the Incarnation*, which has become one of the great classics of Christian literature. Through prayer, study, and the witness of others around him, Athanasius came to a deep grasp of the mystery of God's love revealed through the incarnation of Christ. He was so grateful for what God had done, out of sheer love for his people, that he felt compelled to defend this truth at all costs. In this small book, Athanasius struck at the heart of Christian truth:

> There were thus two things which the Savior did for us by becoming Man. He banished death from us and made us anew; and invisible and imperceptible as in himself he is, he became visible through his works and revealed himself as the Word of the Father, the Ruler and King of the whole creation.

In 313, the Emperor Constantine became a Christian, opening the door for public acceptance of Christianity. As the faith spread throughout the Empire in the fourth century, it became clear that the church needed to protect the gospel by articulating and clarifying what Christians really believed about Jesus and his relationship to the Father. Concerned about the possible rift that could erupt over a growing theological dispute involving the divinity of Christ, Constantine called the bishops to a council in the city of Nicaea in 325. Because of his reputation as a prayerful man and a talented theologian, Athanasius was invited to attend the council with his bishop.

The conflict centered around Arius, a popular priest in the Alexandrian church, who was teaching that, while God the Father is eternal, the Son was not. He had been created by the Father, and so the Word had a beginning and therefore was even subject to change.

Athanasius recognized the danger in such a teaching. If Jesus were merely a creature, then worship of him would be idolatry and the entire purpose of the incarnation—the destruction of death and the gaining of eternal life—would not have been achieved. Such propositions struck at the very heart of the gospel and left people with an empty hope.

The entire controversy was more than an intellectual dispute over philosophical and metaphysical nuances. The Arians acted as a political party, seeking Constantine's favor by trying to destroy those who supported the orthodox position. The council denounced Arius' teachings and sent him into exile. The council also issued a statement of faith in the incarnation—the basis for the Nicene Creed, which is said at Mass today.

The creed proclaims that Jesus Christ, the only Son of God, is "eternally begotten of the Father, God from God, Light from Light, True God from True God, begotten, not made, one in being with the Father." The wording emphasizes that the Father and Son are of the same, uncreated essence (*Homoousion* in Greek), using a terminology which was at the heart of many a controversy, but which Athanasius defended throughout his lifetime.

In his writings, Athanasius often used analogies to help explain the intimate and eternal union that exists between the Father and the Son, such as this one from his "Statement of Faith":

> For like as the well is not a river, nor the river a well, but both are one and the same water which is conveyed in a channel from the well to the river, so the Father's deity passes into the Son without flow and without division. For the Lord says, "I came out from the Father" (John 16:28). But he is ever with the Father, for He is in the bosom of the Father, nor was ever the bosom of the Father void of the deity of the Son.

A Target of the Arians

Athanasius was elected Bishop of Alexandria in 328 and his evident love for the Lord made him extremely popular among his people. Yet because he occupied such an important position in the church and because he so adamantly defended the gospel, he became a constant target of the Arians. In 335, the Arians had regained favor with Constantine and sought—under the guise of a host of ridiculously false charges—to depose Athanasius. He was summoned to a council in Tyre.

One of the charges was that Athanasius had murdered a bishop named Arsenius and kept one of his hands for magical purposes. Actually, the Arians had bribed Arsenius to go into hiding, but he was captured by Athanasius' supporters. He was ushered into the council wrapped up in a cloak. Athanasius turned up the cloak and showed that one hand was still attached, and then, in a moment of suspense, he exposed the other hand! Despite his defense, however, the cards were stacked against him, and Athanasius was exiled to Gaul.

Athanasius returned to Alexandria two years later in 337, after Constantine's death, only to be banished again in 339, when the late emperor's son, Constantius, sided with the Arians. During this exile, which lasted seven years, Athanasius took two monks to Rome with him. Rome's encounter with monasticism, along with Athanasius' immensely popular biography of the Egyptian hermit Anthony, planted the seeds in the West for the monastic tradition that the great St. Benedict would establish almost 200 years later.

Joy at His Return

Athanasius returned to Alexandria in 346 amid great rejoicing by the people, some of whom reportedly walked a hundred miles to greet him. For nearly ten years, Athanasius was able to care for his church at Alexandria in peace, molding it into a model Christian community.

This "golden decade" ended when Athanasius escaped from the soldiers of the pro-Arian Emperor Constantius in 356. For six years, Athanasius hid, moving from the cells of the desert monks to the tombs of kings, sometimes living incognito in the city itself. A legion of his devoted supporters set up a network to keep him safe and disseminate his letters. Some of Athanasius' greatest writings were completed during this period.

The exile ended at Constantius' death in 361, and it seemed as if Athanasius' battles were finally over. Yet he endured two more brief exiles. In 362, the pagan Emperor Julian banished him. As he departed the city, Athanasius calmly told his weeping friends, "Be of good heart, it is only a cloud and will soon pass away." Taking a boat on the Nile toward Upper Egypt, he was pursued by government officers. When the pursuers stopped the boat to ask for news of Athanasius, the bishop himself replied, "He is not far off" and escaped unrecognized.

Athanasius returned to his see in 363 on the occasion of Julian's death. After a fifth exile of only a few months in 365, he spent the last years of his life in peace. By the time Athanasius died in 373, Arianism had been weakened by internal divisions and no longer posed a major threat to the church.

In 381, the Council of Constantinople affirmed the statements from the Council of Nicaea concerning Jesus' divinity. Athanasius' steadfastness and courage had kept the church from straying from the truth—preserving the wonder of Christianity for us in our day. "For who is our joy and boast," Athanasius wrote, "but our Lord and Savior Jesus Christ, who suffered for us, and by himself made known to us the Father."

From St. Athanasius' *On the Incarnation:*

The resurrection of the body to immortality, which results henceforward from the work of Christ, the common Savior and true Life of all, is more effectively proved by facts than by words to those whose mental vision is sound. For, if, as we have shown, death was destroyed and everybody tramples on it because of Christ, how much more did he himself first trample and destroy it in his own body! Death having been slain by him, then, what other issue could there be than the resurrection of his body and its open demonstration as the monument of his victory? How could the destruction of death have been manifested at all, had not the Lord's body been raised?

But if anyone finds even this insufficient, let him find proof of what has been said in present facts. Dead men cannot take effective action; their power of influence on others lasts only till the grave. Deeds and actions that energise others belong only to the living. Well, then, look at the facts in this case. The Saviour is working mightily among men, every day he is invisibly persuading numbers of people all over the world, both within and beyond the Greek-speaking world, to accept his faith and be obedient to his teaching. Can anyone, in face of this, still doubt that he has risen and lives, or rather that he is himself the Life?

Does a dead man prick the consciences of men, so that they throw all the traditions of their fathers to the winds and bow down before the teaching of Christ? If he is no longer active in the world, as he must needs be if he is dead, how is it that he makes the living to cease from their activities, the adulterer from his adultery, the murderer from murdering, the unjust from avarice, while the profane and godless man becomes religious? If he did not rise, but is still dead, how is it that he routs and persecutes and overthrows the false gods, whom unbelievers think to be alive, and the evil spirits whom they worship? For where Christ is named, idolatry is destroyed and the fraud of evil spirits is exposed; indeed, no such spirit can endure that Name, but takes to flight on sound of it. This is the work of one who lives, not of one dead; and, more than that, it is the work of God. It would be absurd to say that the evil spirits whom he drives out and the idols which he destroys are alive, but that he who drives out and destroys, and whom they themselves acknowledge to be Son of God, is dead.

The Life of Athanasius

298 - Born in Alexandria, Egypt, to Christian family

318 - Is ordained a deacon; writes *On the Incarnation*

325 - Attends Council of Nicaea

328 - Elected Bishop of Alexandria

335 - Summoned to Council of Tyre by Arians and exiled to Gaul

337 - Returns to Alexandria

339 - Exiled to Rome when Emperor Constantius sides with Arians

346 - Returns to Alexandria amid great rejoicing

356 - Arian charges against Athanasius are revived; he escapes crowded church service and begins third exile

361 - Returns to assume bishopric

362 - Banished by Emperor Julian. Begins fourth exile in Upper Egypt

363 - Returns to Alexandria after death of Julian

365 - By Emperor's orders, begins fifth exile, which lasts only a few months

373 - Dies in Alexandria

381 - The Council of Constantinople affirms the statements from the Council of Nicaea concerning Jesus' divinity.

The Apostle to Rome

Saint Philip Neri

1515 - 1595

"Ecco Filippone! Here comes the great Philip!" This was a familiar cry in the streets of sixteenth-century Rome as the local youth spotted Philip Neri strolling down the street with his friends in the late afternoon. Philip was hard to miss, with his large white shoes, rough coat, and comical hat.

This was the priest who made them laugh, the one carrying a bunch of weeds and smelling them as if they were roses, the one wearing his clothes inside out. This priest—who brought the joy of the Lord to an entire city—was a much-sought-after confessor by rich and poor alike, who miraculously healed the sick. This was the priest who read joke books before Mass in order to keep from going into ecstasies. This was the priest who, by following the Spirit's promptings, spawned a religious revival and established a new religious congregation.

Yet, when Philip Neri arrived in Rome at the age of eighteen in 1533, he had no plans other than to live the solitary life of a hermit. Moved by the Holy Spirit, he left a potentially lucrative business opportunity and went to a city strewn with the physical debris of recent warfare and the spiritual debris of a church caught up in luxury, intrigue, and political maneuvering.

The Beginning of a Vocation

Philip was a Florentine by birth. His mother died when he was only five years old, and he was raised by a loving step-grandmother. His father—a poor notary—sent Philip at the age of seventeen to live with his cousin in central Italy and become a merchant. The hope was that Philip would inherit the man's business. Philip, however, was more attracted to the nearby Benedictine abbey of Monte Cassino than to his job. He spent many evenings in the abbey's shadows, lost in prayer. Within a short time, he left for Rome, where he intended to live in peace and solitude.

Philip's first few years in Rome were almost totally given over to prayer. Eventually, he sold his books because he couldn't concentrate on anything in the classroom but the crucifix. Often he visited seven famous churches located in various parts of the city. Sometimes he spent the night lying on the floor of one of the churches, immersed in prayer. He loved to pray in the catacombs beneath the Church of San Sebastiano. There in the cool darkness, surrounded by the tombs of the early martyrs, Philip found the perfect environment for contemplating the sweetness of his Lord.

The Fire of the Spirit

It was in these catacombs, on the night before Pentecost 1544, that Philip experienced an extraordinary visitation of God: As he was absorbed in prayer, he saw a ball of fire enter his mouth and travel down to his heart. The sensation of intense heat—the all-consuming fire of God's love—was so great that he threw himself on the ground to cool himself, pleading, "Enough, Lord, enough! I cannot take any more!" The experience not only filled him with joy, it also affected him physically. He would sometimes tremble and shake, and his heart would throb powerfully. The sensation of heat never left him, forcing him to go around with his cassock unbuttoned, even in winter. Many were healed simply by the warmth emanating from his breast.

Just as the heat was constant, so too was the joy of knowing God's presence. Despite his efforts to avoid drawing attention to himself, Philip often found it difficult to hide his fervor. In later life, he often had to lean his elbows on the altar to keep from shaking during Mass. Some said that his entire body lifted off the floor. Yet Philip never thought of himself as better than others. If anything, he became more humble as he reflected on his sin and unworthiness.

As Philip drew closer to God, he was also drawn closer to others. He began to spend time on the streets of Rome, casually striking up conversations with people, looking for opportunities to share the gospel. He soon became a popular figure; his natural charm and joy were hard to resist.

While he was still a layman, Philip began working with different charitable organizations around Rome, caring for the poor in the city's squalid hospitals, ministering to the patients' physical and spiritual needs. One of these organizations—the Confraternity of Charity—was based in the Church of San Girolamo della Carita. It was here that Philip met Fr. Persiano Rosa, who became his spiritual director and close friend. Seeing Philip's talent for caring for people, Rosa pressed him to become a priest, but Philip resisted. He didn't think he deserved such an honor. Finally, out of obedience, he relented. In 1551, at the age of thirty-six, Philip was ordained a priest.

A Wise and Loving Confessor

Philip was immediately drawn to the ministry of reconciliation, and his reputation as an insightful and gifted confessor spread rapidly. Long lines began forming outside his confessional, and Philip would often remain there from daybreak until noon, when he would say Mass. Never wanting anyone to be turned away, Philip left the key to his door under the front mat for those who could only see him during the evening or late at night.

Philip encouraged people to come often, sometimes every day, and he used this regular contact to help guide them into a deeper relationship with God. His wisdom in the confessional was borne of experience and insight into human nature. Noble and wealthy men and women, laborers, merchants, and peasants—all sought him out because, through Philip, they encountered the mercy and compassion of the Lord. He was patient, kind, and sympathetic, leading his penitents to freely unburden themselves of their sins. "Sympathy with those who have fallen is the best way of not falling oneself," he would say.

Less concerned with externals than with matters of the heart, Philip sought to bring Christ's love and healing touch to anyone who came to him. To a woman who asked if she should continue to wear the high-heeled shoes that were fashionable at the time, Philip replied, "Just be careful you don't fall." He told those who wanted difficult penances, "If you absolutely must overdo something, then overdo meekness, obedience, and amiability, because all that is already good in itself." When one man came to confession quite casually, Philip gave him a crucifix, then excused himself. He returned a short time later to find the man in tears, his heart pierced with the knowledge of his sin.

Many times, Philip knew what a person was going to confess before a single word was spoken—leaving the person dumbfounded, humbled, and convinced of God's mercy. He often surprised people with unexpected words and deeds, at one time even slapping a young man to shake him out of his over-scrupulous self-examinations. He sent wealthy people to hospitals to serve the poor and brought the downhearted out of their melancholy by his own joy and cheerfulness. Changing hearts one by one, Philip sparked a renewal in Rome.

The Beginnings of the Oratory

Concerned that the young men of his day were falling into sin through their aimless pursuits after work, Philip invited them to his room to pray, discuss scripture, and study the lives of the saints and church history. Again, to avoid emphasis on externals, he encouraged them to talk from the heart—not in a scholarly, overly pious way. After several hours of prayer, spontaneous sermons, and discussion, the group took walks around the city. They were regularly followed by the curious, the faithful, and the suspicious.

Philip's meetings became so popular that the group—called the "Oratory" or "little chapel"—soon moved to the church's attic where they had more room. As the numbers swelled, the structure of the meetings became somewhat more formal, and some of the talks were prepared beforehand. Philip loved music, and often his beloved *laudi*—popular hymns from Florence—ended the sessions. At one point, the Oratory drew some well-known musicians—including Giovanni Pierluigi da Palestrina.

In addition to his Oratory meetings, Philip continued his visits to the seven churches and soon had hundreds of followers. On Sundays and feast days, outdoor Oratories with music and picnicking attracted as many as 4,000 people. Philip managed to combine recreation and festivity with holiness, and his freedom of expression and humble love for the Lord affected the entire city. His pilgrimage at Lent, for example, proved a powerful antidote to the wild excesses of the Roman Carnival.

Philip's great following attracted the attention of church authorities as well, and the reaction was not always positive. Some were concerned about the practice of permitting laymen to preach sermons, and some protested that laypeople should not receive the sacraments as frequently as Philip advocated. At one point, Pope Paul IV's vicar general ordered Philip to stop hearing confessions—a painful ordeal for him. However, the vicar general died shortly afterward, and the Pope made his peace with Philip. Through all the questions, suspicions, and accusations, Philip maintained an inner peace and prayed for his persecutors.

A Fool for Christ

A community soon grew up around Philip's Oratory, with his devoted followers living out the life of service to others that Philip had initiated. In 1575, Pope Gregory XIII gave the Oratory its own church near the papal court and issued a bull officially establishing it as a congregation. Always the individualist, however, Philip had no thoughts of setting up a conventional order. During the years it took to finalize the rule and government of the congregation, Philip forbade the members from taking vows. Their only bond, he said, should be a bond of love.

As Philip grew older, his eccentric humor came into full force. Insistent that he not be held in awe because of his extraordinary gifts, he took every opportunity to play the fool. Once, at a solemn church ceremony, he went up to a member of the Swiss Guard and playfully tugged on his beard. He sometimes ordered his disciples to carry out similar jokes as a way of teaching them humility and obedience. One of his more famous followers, Francesco Tarugi, was ordered to carry Philip's old dog, Capriccio, during the Oratory's pilgrimages through the streets. When Capriccio died, Tarugi wrote a sonnet celebrating his liberation from the dog.

Much of Philip's last years were spent in solititude and prayer. Daily Mass in his private chapel would often take hours, as he became lost in adoration of the Lord. At times, Philip would be so overcome with love for God that he could scarcely preach.

He was afflicted by poor health for many years and died on May 26, 1595. He was canonized in 1622, along with four of his contemporaries: Ignatius of Loyola, Francis Xavier, Teresa of Avila, and Isidore the Farmer. Romans joked that on that day the Pope canonized four Spaniards and one saint.

By the time of Philip's death, seven oratories had sprung up in Italy, and, in time, Oratorian congregations spread throughout the world. Philip Neri had entered Rome to live a quiet life as a hermit, but the Lord had other plans for him. Known as the "apostle to Rome," Philip left his imprint on his adopted city and on the world by reflecting the love, joy, and humility of Christ.

The Apostle to Rome

The English Cardinal John Henry Newman, who brought the Oratory to England in the nineteenth century, wrote a sermon on "The Mission of St. Philip Neri," parts of which are excerpted here.

You know, my Brethren, what is commonly meant by an Apostle of a country. It means one who converts its heathen inhabitants to the Christian faith, such as St. Augustine of England; accordingly, his proper function is Baptism. Hence you find St. Augustine, St. Patrick, St. Boniface, or St. Francis baptizing their hundreds and thousands. This was the office to which St. Philip wished to minister in India; but . . . he was kept at home for a different work. He was kept at home, in the very heart of Christendom, not to evangelize, but to recover; and his instrument of conversion was, not Baptism, but Penance. The Confessional was the seat and seal of his peculiar Apostolate. Hence, as St. Francis Xavier baptized his tens of thousands, Philip was, every day and almost every hour, for forty-five years, restoring, teaching, encouraging, and guiding penitents along the narrow way of salvation.

We are told in his Life, that "he abandoned every other care, and gave himself to hearing confessions." Not content with the day, he gave up a considerable portion of the night to it also. Before dawn he had generally confessed a good number. When he retired to his room, he still confessed every one who came; though at prayers, though at meals, he broke off instantly, and attended to the call. When the church was opened at daybreak, he went down to the Confessional, and remained in it till noon, when he said

Mass. When no penitents came, he remained near his Confessional; he never intermitted hearing confessions for any illness. . . . It was this extraordinary persevering service in so trying, so wearing a duty, for forty-five years, that enabled him to be the new Apostle of the Sacred City. Thus it was, as the lesson in his Office says, that "he bore innumerable children to Christ." He was ever suffering their miseries, and fighting with their sins, and travailing with their good resolves, year after year, whatever their state of life, their calling, their circumstances, if so be that he might bring them safe to heaven, with a superhuman, heroic patience. . . .

Nothing was too high for him, nothing too low. He taught poor begging women to use mental prayer; he took out boys to play; he protected orphans; he acted as novice-master to the children of St. Dominic. He was the teacher and director of artisans, mechanics, cashiers in banks, merchants, workers in gold, artists, men of science. He was consulted by monks, canons, lawyers, physicians, courtiers; ladies of the highest rank, convicts going to execution, engaged in their turn his solicitude and prayers. Cardinals hung about his room, and Popes asked for his miraculous aid in disease, and his ministrations in death. It was his mission to save men, not from, but in, the world. . . . He, however, was, after all and in all, their true model—the humble priest, shrinking from every kind of dignity, or post, or office, and living the greater part of the day and night in prayer, in his room or upon the housetop.

The Life of Philip Neri

1515 - Born in Florence on Jul. 22

1520 - His mother dies

1532 - Leaves Florence for his cousin's home in San Germano

1533 - Arrives in Rome

1544 - Mystical experience of Holy Spirit in catacombs on eve of Pentecost

1551 - Is ordained a priest; is drawn to ministry of the confessional

1553 - Begins pilgrimages to seven churches

1554 - Beginning of the Oratory

1558 - Oratory moves to larger quarters in attic of Church of San Girolamo

1559 - Pope Paul IV's vicar general investigates Philip's activities

1564 - The Congregation of the Oratory begins to take shape

1567 - Suspicious of Oratory, Pope Pius V sends spies but takes no action

1575 - Pope Gregory XIII issues bull establishing the Oratory as a congregation

1579 - Oratories modeled after Philip's spring up in other Italian cities

1583 - Moves from San Girolamo to congregation's new church

1595 - Dies on May 26

Giraudon/Art Resource, NY

A Bridge Between Heaven and Earth

Saint Catherine of Siena

1347 - 1380

Lapa Benincasa's shrieks bounced off the walls of her kitchen and into the narrow streets of Siena. Her daughter Catherine, the twenty-fourth of her twenty-five children, had just shaved her head. The fifteen-year-old was adamant that she not be married off, and to show the seriousness of her intention, she had chopped off her hair.

Strong wills prevailed on both sides. Catherine's mother and father, Giacomo, punished their daughter for her disobedience. She was put to work as the household maid, and her room was taken away from her so that she could not pray.

But Catherine loved to pray. As a small child, she imitated the pious practices of the Dominican Friars down the hill from her home. In 1352, when she was only six years old, she saw a vision of Jesus above the Church of San Domenico, accompanied by the apostles Peter, John, and Paul. At the tender age of seven, she vowed to remain single and dedicated her life to God.

Catherine's parents insisted she be married, and for a time, Catherine went along with the parties and festive attire that her married sister Bonaventura encouraged. But when Bonaventura died in childbirth, Catherine resumed her original vow. Nothing her parents said or did would change her mind. She gladly served them, and, amid the bustle of a busy household, practiced building a cell within herself in which she could enjoy the sweetness of the Lord.

The family was baffled; her brothers taunted her. But one day while Catherine was kneeling in a corner praying, Giacomo saw a white dove appear over her head. He saw it as a sign from God. Catherine was a special girl, and she would be given her own room and permitted to live as she wished.

With characteristic intensity and single-mindedness, Catherine plunged into a life of fasting, prayer, and penance. Her growing passion for Christ made her desire to enter into his own suffering on the cross, so she took a vow of silence, left the house only to go to Mass, practiced severe fasts and corporal punishments, and deprived herself of sleep. Even for the fourteenth century, Catherine's penances were harsh, and since she was not in a convent, there was no superior to temper them. Lapa was beside herself. "Daughter, I see you dying before my eyes," she sobbed.

A Mystical Marriage

As Catherine grew weaker from the demands she placed on her body, her spirit soared. Jesus made himself known to her in visions and words, and she often saw and spoke with

Mary and the saints. Raymond of Capua, Catherine's close friend and her third and final spiritual director, said at one point that the revelations Catherine told him seemed so extraordinary that he began to doubt she was telling the truth. While he was thinking these thoughts, he looked at her face and instead saw the majestic face of a bearded man he suspected was Christ. Terrified, he asked, "Who are you?" The man replied, "He who is." At these words, Raymond again saw Catherine's face, but his vision of the face of Christ put an immediate end to his doubts.

Catherine's intimate conversations with the Lord eventually led to a "mystical marriage." In a vision in 1368, Catherine was presented to Jesus by Mary and given a ring which only she could see. This "marriage," however, would end Catherine's seclusion. The Lord began to call her to a more public life so she could reap souls for her Spouse.

Catherine was horrified—she wanted to stay within the walls of her cell—and protested that as a member of the "weaker" sex, she would be unable to go out into a world in which women were expected to stay hidden and at home. The Lord responded, "In my eyes there is neither male or female, rich or poor, but all are equal, for I can do all things with equal ease." God had chosen Catherine, he told her, to chastise proud and learned men.

Re-entering the World

This twenty-one-year-old woman who had kept silent for so many years had to learn to be among people again, loving them as she loved Christ. She began by attending family dinners. Several years earlier, in 1365, she had taken the habit of a group of Dominican sisters known as the *mantellate*, who lived in their own homes and performed charitable works. Now, like the *mantellate*, she threw herself wholeheartedly into caring for the poor and sick.

As her spiritual wisdom became known, her isolation ended, and she soon became immersed in the world. Men and women flocked to hear her spiritual insights. Eventually a group of disciples assembled around her, calling her "mother" even though many were older than she. These were her dear friends whom she loved intensely. Many of them stayed with her until her death.

Not all were enamored with Catherine, however; some mocked her and spread vicious rumors about her. Even some of the Dominican friars at the church were annoyed because she sometimes wept loudly during Mass and nearly always went into long ecstasies—in which she would remain rigid and senseless—after taking Communion.

Despite her more active life, the Lord remained close to Catherine. Taking care of an old woman with a festering sore, Catherine became nauseated. Upbraiding herself for her revulsion, she drank the water she had used to wash the sore. She later told Raymond, "Never in my life have I tasted any food and drink sweeter or more exquisite." To reward her for this act, the Lord drew her towards the wound in his own side and allowed her to drink his blood. After this experience, Catherine was gradually unable to digest any type of food and often existed only on the Eucharist.

In another vision, the Lord exchanged his heart for hers; in still another, she received the painful wounds of Christ, but at Catherine's request, they were invisible to all but her. In 1370, during a grave illness, she experienced a "mystical death." For four hours, she appeared dead and experienced the joys of heaven. But these mystical experiences, instead of drawing her away from the world, drew her more deeply into it.

Catherine's Political Struggles

Catherine's circle of influence had already begun to widen. When the plague broke out in Siena in 1374, news spread of her courage and healing touch. When one of her friends came down with the infection, she told him, "Get up. This is no time for lying in a soft bed!" He immediately recovered. Her growing reputation brought her invitations to other cities. In Pisa and elsewhere, she preached so effectively that several priests had to accompany her to hear the confessions of repentant sinners. In several cases, Catherine prayed for hardened criminals who then repented before their executions.

In Catherine's time, many in the clergy had been corrupted by wealth and temporal power. Catherine prayed continuously for Church reform and wrote scores of letters to high church officials, exhorting them to root out corruption and choose virtuous men for church offices. She was never afraid to say what she thought and frankly told heads of state and rulers what she believed was God's will for them. To one fallen-away priest, she wrote: "Those who should be the temples of God are the stables of swine."

Neither was she shy about telling the Florentines to stay loyal to Pope Gregory XI, in spite of the mounting tension between Florence and the papacy. To Catherine, the pope's position as head of the church made him "sweet Christ on earth." In 1376, the Florentines asked Catherine to go to Avignon in France, where the popes had resided since 1309, to act as mediator. The peace mission failed because Florence had no real intention of reconciling. However, Catherine developed an affectionate relationship with Gregory—whom she called "Babbo Mio"—and succeeded in persuading him to return to Rome, a move she believed would restore peace and strengthen the papacy.

Yet the state of the church continued to decline in the last years of her life. Pope Gregory died and was replaced by Pope Urban VI. Catherine begged Urban to treat his enemies mercifully: "Mingle mercy with justice, lest your justice become unjust." It was to no avail. Urban alienated the French clergy so much that they declared the papal election invalid and elected their own pope.

Urban wanted Catherine in Rome for spiritual support, and in 1378, she and twenty-two of her disciples arrived there. Even the citizens of Rome were turning against the pontiff. Catherine saw this as a great sin, and begged the Lord to forgive them and to allow her to suffer the punishment they deserved. She was tormented by evil spirits and grew weaker physically. However, she continued a daily one-mile walk to St. Peter's for Mass until finally, she could no longer leave her bed. She died on April 29, 1380, at the age of thirty-three. The papal schism that Catherine mourned so deeply was to continue another forty-four years, until 1424.

The Dialogue

In addition to hundreds of letters, Catherine left the world a great classic of Christian literature. Before her death,

Catherine dictated a "book" to one of her secretaries while she was in ecstasy, which became known as *The Dialogue*. Through a conversation between God and a "soul," Catherine revealed the depth of the Lord's love and mercy.

She described Christ as a bridge between heaven and earth, which each soul must climb in order to escape from drowning in the river below. There are three stairs on this bridge: the first stair is the feet of Christ nailed to the cross, which symbolizes the stage where souls are fearful of the consequences of sin and try to find God out of slavish fear; the second is Christ's side, from which souls can see his heart and realize how tremendously they are loved by God; the third stair is Christ's mouth, where souls now love perfectly and find peace from the war they waged against sin.

Catherine's life was also a bridge—from the Lord to us. She who experienced the intensity of divine love and mercy responded in kind, not only to God, but to those around her—from poor peasant to powerful king. From the wisdom she received from the Lord, her writings continue to teach us—a recognition made official in 1970, when Pope Paul VI made Catherine a Doctor of the Church.

Catherine wrote this letter to Pope Gregory XI in Avignon, France, in 1376. She refers to Gregory's plan to send mercenary troops against rebellious Italian cities and begs him to act on his intenton to return to Rome.

In the name of Christ crucified and of gentle Mary. Revered father in Christ gentle Jesus,

I Caterina, your unworthy daughter, servant and slave of the servants of Jesus Christ, am writing to you in his precious blood. I long to see you a courageous man, free of slavish fear, learning from the good gentle Jesus, whose vicar you are. Such was his boundless love for us that he ran to the shameful death of the cross heedless of torment, shame, insult, and outrage. He suffered them all, totally free of fear, such was his hungry desire for the Father's honor and our salvation. For love had made him completely let go of himself, humanly speaking. Now this is just what I want you to do, father. Let go of yourself wherever selfish love is concerned. Do not love yourself selfishly, nor others selfishly, but love yourself and your neighbors for God's sake and God for his own sake, since he is worthy of love, and since he is supreme eternal good. Take as your example this slain Lamb, for the blood of this Lamb will give you courage for every battle. In the blood you will lose all fear, and you will become a good shepherd who will lay down your life for your little sheep.

Up then, father; don't sit still any longer! Fire yourself with tremendous desire, expecting divine help and providence. For it seems to me that divine Goodness is about to turn the great wolves into lambs. This is why I am coming there soon, to lay them in your lap, humbled. I am certain that you, as their father, will receive them in spite of their persecution and injustice against you. You will learn from gentle First Truth, who says that the good shepherd, once he has found the little lost sheep, will put it on his shoulders and take it back to the fold. So do that, father. Once your little lost sheep has been found, take it on love's shoulders and put it in the fold of holy Church. . . . As for the soldiers you have hired to come here, hold them back and don't let them come, for they would ruin everything instead of setting things right.

My dear father, you ask me about your coming. I answer you in the name of Christ crucified: come as soon as you can. If you can, come before September, and if you cannot come earlier, don't delay beyond the end of September. Pay no attention to any opposition but like a courageous and fearless man, come! And, as you value your life, see that you don't come with an army, but with the cross in your hand, as a meek lamb. If you do, you will fulfill God's will. But if you come in any other way you will be violating that will rather than fulfilling it. Be glad, father! Be jubilant! Come! Come!

I'll say no more. Keep living in God's holy and tender love. Gentle Jesus! Jesus love!

Pardon me, father. I humbly ask your dear blessing.

The Life of Catherine of Siena

1347 - Born in Siena to Lapa and Giacomo Benincasa, the twenty-fourth of twenty-five children

1352 - Has first vision of Jesus above the church of San Domenico

1353 - Takes vow of virginity

1365 - Takes the Dominican habit and enters three-year period of prayer, penance, and seclusion in her parents' house

1368 - Has a vision in which she is mystically espoused to Jesus; re-enters the world

1370 - Experiences a "mystical death"

1374 - Nurses the sick during plague in Siena

1375 - Visits Pisa to preach; receives the stigmata while there

1376 - Travels to Avignon and persuades Pope Gregory XI to return to Rome

1378 - Finishes dictating *The Dialogue*; moves to Rome at the request of Pope Urban VI

1380 - Dies in Rome on Apr. 29

Acknowledgements

Page 15 Excerpt taken from *The Diary of Sister M. Faustina Kowalska, Divine Mercy in My Soul*, copyright© 1987, Congregation of Marians of the Immaculate Conception, Stockbridge, MA 01263. All world rights reserved. Reprinted with permission.

Page 25 Translation of St. Bernard of Clairvaux's writings by Kilian Walsh, O.C.S.O. and Irene Edmonds. Reprinted with permission of Cistercian Publications, Kalamazoo, Mich.

Page 66 Letter reprinted with permission of Simon & Schuster from *Letters and Papers from Prison*, Revised, Enlarged edition by Dietrich Bonhoeffer, translated by Reginald Fuller, Frank Clark et al. Copyright© 1953, 1967, 1971 by SCM Press, Ltd.

Page 94 Takashi Nagai's funeral address taken from *The Bells of Nagasaki*, by Takashi Nagai, translated by William Johnston, English translation copyright© 1984 by Kodansha International Ltd. Reprinted by permission. All rights reserved.

Page 110 Excerpt taken from *The Science of the Cross*, by Edith Stein, Copyright© 1960 by Regnery Publishing. All rights reserved. Reprinted by special permission of Regnery Publishing Inc., Washington, D.C.

Page 123 Excerpt taken from *To Love Christ Jesus*, by St. Alphonsus Liguori, edited by Nancy Fearon, I.H.M. and Christopher Farrell, C.SS.R. Published by Liguori Press; originally published by the Sisters, Servants of the Immaculate Heart of Mary, Monroe, Mich. Used by permission of the editor.

Page 136 Excerpt taken from *Jeanne Jugan* by Paul Milcent, translated by Alan Neame, published and copyright© 1980 by Darton, Longman and Todd, Ltd., London. Used by permission of the publishers.

Page 146 Clare's letter taken from *Francis and Clare, The Complete Works*, translation and introduction by Regis J. Armstrong, O.F.M., copyright© 1982 by the Missionary Society of St. Paul the Apostle in the State of New York. Published by Paulist Press. Used by permission of Paulist Press.

Page 161 Excerpt taken from *Give Me Souls! Life of Don Bosco*, by Peter Lappin. Copyright© 1986 by Salesiana Publishers. Used by Permission.

Page 172 Letter taken from *Katharine Drexel, A Biography*, by Sister Consuela Marie Duffy, S.B.S., copyright© 1966 The Sisters of the Blessed Sacrament. Used by permission.

Page 184 Selection taken from *On the Incarnation* by St. Athanasius, published by St. Vladimir's Press, Crestwood, N.Y. Used by permission.